The Secret Christmas

KW-757-792

The Secret Christmas

Edited by
FIONA MACMATH

Foreword by
HRH Princess Alexandra

Darton, Longman and Todd
London

First published in Great Britain in 1990 by
Darton, Longman and Todd Ltd
89 Lillie Road, London SW6 1UD

Introduction and arrangement
© 1990 Fiona MacMath

British Library Cataloguing in Publication Data

The Secret Christmas.
 1. English literature. Special subjects: Christmas.
Anthologies
 I. MacMath, Fiona
 820.8033

ISBN 0–232–51907–2

All royalties earned by the sale
of this book are being given to
Crisis, 212 Whitechapel Road, London

Phototypeset by Input Typesetting Ltd, London SW19 8DR
Printed and bound in Great Britain by
Courier International Ltd, Tiptree, Essex

Dedicated to

Lynne Woodward
Kath and Mike Power
Peter and Anne Templeman
Simon and Joy Parke
Claire and Gerard Disbrey
Helen and Ian Mylam
Elizabeth Vinten Pinner

for keeping open doors all the year round

Contents

Foreword

I would like to commend this book and the thoughtful excerpts which have been put together.

It certainly conveys a variety of vivid pictures of Christmas and I wish Crisis well in their work.

May you all have a very happy Christmas.

Alexandra

PATRON

Introduction

Most people keep two Christmases – one blazing with greens, reds and gold, a public-spirited, family affair, for which whole factories labour all year round to provide the paper Santa Clauses, crackers, displays and designs for every conceivable domestic item at Christmas time. It is the Christmas the new employers, the Puritans, banned as an uncommercial proposition – their gifts of prophecy failed them here – and an undignified, unholy row. It is the Christmas we love to hate, complete with a hundred horrid chores, unwanted relations and Bing Crosby crooning in every department store.

The other Christmas is secret – blue and silvery white for those who have the eyes for that kind of thing, but for most, a fleeting sense of joy and wonder which touches them when the horror of the office party is safely over, and when there is an oasis of quiet in the family celebrations: midnight mass; the King's College service of Nine Lessons and Carols on the radio; the first glimpse of the Christmas tree in all its glory. It provides the impulse for crusty business men to find small change for the caterwauling urchins carolling at their front doors, and keeps the weary housewives trudging through their preparations.

This is not to say that the first kind of Christmas is not immense fun, but only to say that the second is more precious, and it is what gives the first its joy. If the unimaginably great power behind the universe could love us so much as to become one of us, not in spirit only, but with all the limitations and narrowness that constrain us in our finite, human bodies – then we are loved indeed. To put it in Christian terms: if God could choose freely to become a human – who happened to be a man called Jesus, or Joshua, son of a carpenter, born in a stable, living in an occupied, backward country – then humans are infinitely valuable.

For those who cannot hold God within such a humanly recognizable form, then still, there is a sense that at Christmas, humanity becomes lovable. The claims of the poor, the cold, the homeless, the sad, demand relief. A charity like Crisis (formerly Crisis at Christmas) tugs at people's heartstrings because it is indeed a crisis if at Christmas, of all times, there is hunger and homelessness. Christmas is a celebration of our worth and preciousness – if not to God, then to each other.

Crisis properly means not 'emergency' – a problem to which we must make a response. The true meaning of the word is 'turning point' – a choice we must make. Christmas comes at the turning point of the year; it marks the turning point in God's relations with us. It is a yearly reminder of the choices we are continually forced to make between loving or refusing to love; accepting or refusing to accept. The work of Crisis is not over at Christmas, of course, and nor are our own opportunities to love the people around us. But Christmas – like the baby in the manger – makes ideas of love tangible, and translates them into presents of our time, skills and money.

This collection of prose and poetry for Christmas holds these two themes in mind: the secret, private response of people to Christmas, and the impulse to give which lies at the heart of Christmas, remembering as it does, the gift of God himself to us. There are a few sad and distressing pieces; the Christmas message brings joy to the world, but Christmas itself can heighten the wretchedness of some human circumstances. It promises goodwill from God to all people and between all men and women on earth; that promise is still to be brought to perfect fruition.

We trace the celebration of Christmas from the first faint stirrings of hope in Advent, through the twelve days, New Year, the Epiphany, and on to Candlemas on 2 February. In medieval England, the twelve days were a general holiday, with the women going back to routine work only on 7 January or Distaff Day, and the men on the first Monday after that – Plough Monday. But the Christmas season continued until Candlemas, with reflections on Mary, the Purification, the flight into Egypt, and the childhood of Jesus. I hope this book will give you pleasure over the Christmas season, and make some contribution to the work of Crisis as well.

1

Advent

Advent Prayer

O Lord, again with the turning of the year we begin our pilgrimage toward Christmas. Our hearts as ever rejoice in the glad tidings of Christ who is born in Bethlehem to be the Saviour of all the world. Yet with all our joy, and the long centuries behind us of hearts made glad by His coming, we know there is much in us that deafens our ears to the sound of angel anthems, much that blinds us to the sight of guiding stars amid the darkness, much that crowds our hearts and minds, leaving little room for the humbler benedictions of this life. If repentance can purify our hope, if for this season we may become pure hearted, if now we can welcome you with all our soul, then grace us with your most wondrous blessing through Christ who was born to be the light of the world forever.

ANONYMOUS

Come, lovely Name!

Come, lovely Name; life of our hope!
Lo, we hold our hearts wide ope!
Unlock thy cabinet of day,
Dearest Sweet, and come away,
  Lo, how the thirsty lands
Gasp for thy golden showers, with long-stretched hands!
  Lo, how the labouring earth
  That hopes to be
  All heaven by thee,
  Leaps at thy birth! . . .

Come, royal Name; and pay the expense
Of all this precious patience;
  O come away,
And kill the death of this delay.
And see so many worlds of barren years
Melted and measured out in seas of tears.
O see the weary lids of wakeful hope
(Love's eastern windows) all wide ope
  With curtains drawn,
To catch the day-break of thy dawn.

RICHARD CRASHAW

Advent

I saw him with flesh all be-spread: He came from East.
I saw him with blood all be-shed: He came from West.
I saw that many he with him brought: He came from South.
I saw that the world of him ne rought: He came from North.

'I come from the wedlock as a sweet spouse that have my wife
with me y-nome.
I come from fight as a stalwart knight that my foe have
overcome.
I come from the cheaping as a rich chapman that mankind have
y-bought.
I come from an uncouth land as a silly pilgrim that far have
y-sought.'

ANONYMOUS

---

of him ne rought: cared nothing for him; *y-nome*: taken; *cheaping*: market;
chapman: merchant; *uncouth*: unknown; *silly*: simple

Christmas is coming . . .

There is no more dangerous or disgusting habit than that of celebrating Christmas before it comes, as I am doing in this article. It is the very essence of a festival that it breaks upon one brilliantly and abruptly, that at one moment the great day is not and the next moment the great day is. Up to a certain specific instant you are feeling ordinary and sad; for it is only Wednesday. At the next moment your heart leaps up and your soul and body dance together like lovers; for in one burst and blaze it has become Thursday. I am assuming (of course) that you are a worshipper of Thor, and that you celebrate his day once a week, possibly with human sacrifice. If, on the other hand, you are a modern Christian Englishman, you hail (of course) with the same explosion of gaity the appearance of the English Sunday. But I say that whatever the day is that is to you festive or symbolic, it is essential that there should be a quite clear black line between it and the time going before. And all the old wholesome customs in connection with Christmas were to the effect that one should not touch or see or know or speak of something before the actual coming of Christmas Day. Thus, for instance, children were never given their presents until the actual coming of the appointed hour. The presents were kept tied up in brown-paper parcels, out of which the arm of a doll or the leg of a donkey sometimes accidentally stuck. I wish this principle were adopted in respect of modern Christmas ceremonies and publications. Especially it ought to be observed in connection with what are called the Christmas numbers of magazines. The editors of the magazines bring out their Christmas numbers so long before the time that the reader is more likely to be still lamenting for the turkey of last year than to have seriously settled down to a solid anticipation of the turkey which is to come. Christmas numbers of magazines ought to be tied up in brown paper and kept for Christmas Day. On consideration, I should favour the editors being tied up in brown paper. Whether the leg or arm of an editor should ever be allowed to protrude, I leave to individual choice.

G K CHESTERTON
The Illustrated London News, 29 December 1906

Preparations at Lulling

With only a fortnight to go before Christmas Day, Lulling people were beginning to bestir themselves about their shopping. London might start preparing for the festival at the end of October; Lulling refused to be hustled. October and November had jobs of their own in plenty. December, and the later part of that, was the proper time to think of Christmas, and the idea of buying cards and presents before then was just plain silly.

'Who wants to think of Christmas when there's the autumn digging to do?' said one practically.

'Takes all the gilt off the gingerbread to have Christmas thrown down your throat before December,' agreed another.

But now all the good folk were ready for it, and the shops did a brisk trade. Baskets bulged, and harassed matrons struggled along the crowded main street bearing awkward objects like tricycles and pairs of stilts, flimsily wrapped in flapping paper. Children kept up a shrill piping for the tawdry knick-knacks which caught their eye, and fathers gazed speculatively at train sets and wondered if their two-year-old sons and daughters would be a good excuse to buy one.

At the corner of the Market Square stood Puddocks', the stationers, and here, one windy afternoon, Ella Bembridge was engaged in choosing Christmas cards.

Normally, Ella designed her own Christmas card. It was usually a wood cut or a lino cut, executed with her habitual vigour and very much appreciated by her friends. But somehow, this year, Ella had not done one. So many things had pressed upon her time. There were far more visits these days, both from the rector and from his friend Harold Shoesmith, and the vague unhappiness which hung over her at the thought of change had affected Ella more than she realized. Today, in Puddocks', reduced to turning over their mounds of insipid cards, Ella felt even more depressed.

But, depressed as she was, she set about her appointed task with energy. She made directly towards the section marked 'Cards 6d., 9d., and 1s.' and began a swift process of elimination. Ballet dancers, ponies, dogs, anyone in a crinoline or a beaver hat, were out. So were contrived scenes of an open Bible before a stained-glass window flanked with a Christmas rose or a

7

candle. It was amazing how little was left after this ruthless pruning. Ella, coming up for air, looked at the throng around her to see how others were faring.

She envied the stout woman at her elbow who picked up all the cards embellished with sparkling stuff and read the verses intently. She had plenty of choice. She admired the way in which a tall thin man selected black and white line drawings of Ely Cathedral, Tower Bridge and Bath Abbey with extreme rapidity. She watched, with bitter respect, a large female who forced her way to the desk and demanded the ten dozen printed Christmas cards ordered on August 22nd, and promised faithfully for early December. Here was efficiency, thought Ella, returning to her rummaging.

MISS READ
Winter in Thrush Green

Lady Selecting Her Christmas Cards

Fastidiously, with gloved and careful fingers,
  Through the marked samples she pursues her search,
Which shall it be: the snowscape's wintry langours
  Complete with church,

An urban skyline, children sweetly pretty
  Sledding downhill, the chaste, ubiquitous wreath,
Schooner or candle or the simple Scottie
  With verse underneath?

Perhaps it might be better to emblazon
  With words alone the stiff, punctilious square.
(Oh, not Victorian, certainly. This season
  One meets it everywhere.)

She has a duty proper to the weather –
  A Birth she must announce, a rumour to spread,
Wherefore the very spheres once sang together
  And a star shone overhead.

Here are the Tidings which the shepherds panted
  One to another, kneeling by their flocks.
And they will bear her name (engraved, not printed),
  Twelve-fifty for the box.

PHYLLIS MCGINLEY

Old-fashioned Christmas Cards

It was truly an intoxicating sight! There they lay, in all the glory of painted picture, of tinsel ribbon, of frost that sparkled like the hoar-frost on the glittering fleece of snow on the lawn. We gazed entranced at robins with wide-open beaks, singing songs we could hear in imagination, at flowers whose scent seemed to pour into the air, at plum puddings we could almost taste. There were pictures of the Holy Family in the Stable, with Ox and Ass, and Wise Men offering gifts, and churches that lighted up when we held them to the window, and coaches driving up to inn doors. There were pictures of snow and icicles and holly. It was a heavenly box of delights, and we turned the cards over with cries of excitement.

To children who had few picture-books, who had never been to a picture gallery, who seldom even visited a shop, this was a feast of art. We were hungry for such things. We could never finish looking at them and pointing out their beauties to one another and to our mother . . .

On Christmas morning we had the pleasure of getting cards ourselves. They came on the Day, not a fortnight before, for there was no posting early for Christmas. The postmaster himself brought them through the wood and stayed for a glass of home-made wine. The brown-paper parcels were sealed with scarlet sealing-wax. The letters and cards were in snowy envelopes, and we opened them and passed them round before we went to church. Those with no writing were kept to be sent away. There was a coldness about a Christmas card with no handwriting on it.

We examined our cards closely, we loved them deeply, we kept them for years. When the servant-girl could be persuaded to make a bowl of flour-paste we put some in the scrap-books on Sunday afternoons. Others went into the doll's-house on the shelf of the candlestick cupboard, to be used as bedscreens. The luxury cards with silk fringes, which were occasionally sent to my mother, were carefully placed in my own kitchen drawer of treasures, where they stayed for many years. They took my breath away by their loveliness as I pondered over them and showed them to my friends.

I came across one of my old scrap-books lately. It held the

choicest treasures of childhood, and as I turned the heavy pages I felt again the emotions of rapture and exquisite delight I knew when I was seven or eight; as if those bespangled cards with their robins and snow had kept the essence of childhood in their folded leaves. The cards were so familiar after the long scrutiny to which I had subjected them in those early days that not only every detail appeared fresh, but I remembered the feelings I had once experienced when I looked at them.

Our minds are photographic plates on which childhood impressions are printed, and trifles such as a breath of honeysuckle, an air of music, an old Christmas card, can send us back, can develop that plate. We can return to the stream of consciousness in which we once moved.

ALISON UTTLEY
Country Things

The Christmas Cards

Still it persists, the myth of snow at Christmas,
Unashamedly across all our cards;
Not a few flakes but deep drifts –
Villages cosily half buried in it,
Trees, it would seem, gladly bearing its weight,
Edwardian women wrapped in furs and skating,
Santa Claus showing us the story of the Father
For ever offering the marvellous unattainable gift,
Piercing a way through darkness to the hearth.

The Nativity may be ignored but new life is hoped for.
About this the cheap cards are surely right.
For white is everybody's secret emblem:
We half perceive the meaning of the virgin snow.

SISTER MARY LAURENCE

Snow in Bethlehem

This is written amid fields of snow within a few days of Christmas. And when last I saw snow it was within a few miles of Bethlehem. The coincidence will serve as a symbol of something I have noticed all my life, though it is not very easy to sum up. It is generally the romantic thing that turns out to be the real thing, under the extreme test of realism. It is the sceptical and even rational legend that turns out to be entirely legendary. Everything I had been taught or told led me to regard snow in Bethlehem as a paradox, like snow in Egypt. Every rumour of realism, every indirect form of rationalism, every scientific opinion taken on authority and at third hand, had led me to regard the country where Christ was born solely as a sort of semi-tropical place with nothing but palm-trees and parasols. It was only when I actually looked at it that it looked exactly like a Christmas card.

G K CHESTERTON
The Illustrated London News, 1920

Journey to Bethlehem

It was, as I have said, just like any other road in Palestine. But there was one thing that marked it out from all other roads in the world. It was the road to Bethlehem . . .

. . . And as I went to Bethlehem I remembered a place hushed in snow where shepherds wrapped in thick cloaks watched their flocks under the frosty stars. There was a little shelter in this place in which beasts stamped in their stalls and blew the fog of their breath into the cold air. On the straw near the mangers, sitting in exquisite detachment, was a Mother with a gold circle about her head and a little Child. The stars shone coldly, and through the air came a sound of far-off bells.

I knew perfectly well that this picture was edged with gilt. It was my own private little vision of Bethlehem, something that has been with me all my life, something made up in my mind from Christmas cards sent to me when I was a child, from pictures that I loved before I could read, something formed by the piety and reverence which a cold northern land has cast round the story of the Nativity. Every Christian nation has translated the story of Christ into its own idiom and cradled Him in its own barns. The great mediaeval painters, each man in his own way, painted in the national background of his own country and his own time. And we who came from Europe to Palestine come from an enchanted country to the bare rocks and crags of reality.

I walked along in the airless heat, sorry to say farewell to this little picture of mine; and the heat of the white road to Bethlehem quivered like fire over the limestone walls and beat like the breath of a furnace upon the grey little olive trees and shone through the greenness of the uncurling fig leaves . . .

H V MORTON
In the Steps of the Master

Preparing for Christmas

The Christmas season is domestic; and for that reason most people now prepare for it by struggling in tramcars, standing in queues, rushing away in trains, crowding despairingly into tea-shops, and wondering when or whether they will ever get home. I do not know whether some of them disappear for ever in the toy department or simply lie down and die in the tea-rooms; but by the look of them, it is quite likely. Just before the great festival of the home the whole population seems to have become homeless. It is the supreme triumph of industrial civilisation that, in the huge cities which seem to have far too many houses, there is a hopeless shortage of housing. For a long time past great numbers of our poor have become practically nomadic. We even confess the fact; for we talk of them as Street Arabs. But this domestic institution, in its present ironical phase, has gone beyond such normal abnormality. The feast of the family turns the rich as well as the poor into vagabonds. They are so scattered over the bewildering labyrinth of our traffic and our trade, that they sometimes cannot even reach the tea-shop; it would be indelicate, of course, to mention the tavern. They have a difficulty in crowding into their hotels, let alone separating to reach their houses. I mean quite the reverse of irreverence when I say that their only point of resemblance to the archetypal Christmas family is that there is no room for them at the inn.

G K CHESTERTON
The Thing

Advent Carol

If ye would hear the angels sing
  'Peace on earth and mercy mild',
  Think of him who was once a child,
On Christmas Day in the morning.

If ye would hear the angels sing,
  Rise, and spread your Christmas fare;
  'Tis merrier still the more that share,
On Christmas Day in the morning.

Rise, and bake your Christmas bread;
  Christians, rise! the world is bare,
  And blank, and dark with want and care,
Yet Christmas comes in the morning.

If ye would hear the angels sing,
  Rise, and light your Christmas fire;
  And see that ye pile the logs still higher
On Christmas Day in the morning.

Rise, and light your Christmas fire;
  Christians, rise! the world is old,
  And Time is weary, and worn, and cold,
Yet Christmas comes in the morning.

If ye would hear the angels sing,
  Christians! see ye let each door
  Stand wider than it e'er stood before,
On Christmas Day in the morning.

Rise, and open wide the door;
  Christians, rise! the world is wide,
  And many there be that stand outside,
Yet Christmas comes in the morning.

DORA GREENWELL

Christmas Boxes

Long before Christmas there was a festive spirit abroad in the villages. The month was a season of surprises, and we all prepared some kind of treat for one another. There was a universal giving of presents, which had its culmination on Christmas Day.

Shopkeepers thought of their customers, and to encourage their patronage, and also from feelings of goodwill and kindness, they sent Christmas-boxes. The gifts came with unfailing regularity through the years. We should have thought something was very much wrong with a grocer's store if nothing had come, but every gift was received with delight and thankfulness, however simple it might be. Even the tiniest shops, with bow-window and deep step down to a dark little room, made their small gift at Christmas . . .

Each month the traveller called on us for orders, and this was an important occasion. He sat at the kitchen table, and discussed with my mother all the good things in the shop, and the prices. Then he talked of cricket in summer, for he was in the team, or of shooting in winter, and he told us the news of villages and hamlets in the far valleys and over the hills where he went.

When he drove to the house with the Christmas order there was a Christmas-box for us. Sometimes it was a bottle of port wine, which was sipped on Christmas day. Sometimes it was an ornamental tin casket with about two pounds of mixed dessert biscuits. Even the scent of them was deliciously like roses, and we gazed with rapture when the box was unlatched for us to see. There were little biscuits in the shapes of walnuts and almond-shells, with all the delicate convolutions of the nuts. The shape was very important, it seemed to change the texture of the biscuit. Then there were sugared diamonds, iced with rosy carmine on one side, white on the other, and balls of sweetness with a coriander seed inside, and dominoes with black spots on white ivory, and red strawberries made of marzipan, and ratafias with pink iced centres. These biscuits, in their fine box, were kept locked up in my mother's drawer for great occasions, and eaten sparingly so that they lasted for several weeks. We felt very rich when we nibbled them.

From another shop came a pair of coloured wax candles, which we fitted into the brass candlesticks projecting from the front of the piano. Round each candle was a tiny fluted green glass saucer to catch the drops of wax. It tinkled against the candlestick when the piano was played, the candle-flames fluttered and swung in the wind, and the hot wax rolled slowly down to the glass. It was a pleasure to play waltzes and mazurkas by the light of a Christmas-box of green candles.

The music was often a Christmas-box, too. When I saw the thin white roll of music paper among the loaves of bread, the packages and parcels in the market-basket brought in from the cart, I rushed off at once to the piano. Music was to me the most welcome of the little Christmas surprises that came from the villages. Grocers, confectioners, pork butchers, sent sheets of music with carol and sentimental song . . .

We gave our own produce as Christmas-boxes to those who had worked for us. Rabbits were shot and sent by train to the milk dealer. The postman had a couple, also the roadman, and the porter and station-master. Apples and mince-pies, brawns, rich and spicy, medicine bottles full of cream went here and there in my mother's small basket – the basket decorated with bands of cream straw-plaiting, threaded through the brown.

There was an interchange of mince-pies between friends. The housekeeper at the Castle sent from her storeroom a few mince-pies, very small and puffy and delicate. They were for gentlefolk, and as we tasted them we could see them served on silver dishes to the Squire's company. Our own mince-pies were large, and bursting with mincemeat. We made scores of mince-pies in patty-pans of antique mould, and the mincemeat came from the big stone jar which stood on the pantry bench. Everybody had to eat one at Christmas – carol singers, guisers, even the beggar who came to the door, and the pedlar with his pack. There was friendly criticism of the mince-pies we received from the houses of our friends. We made our wishes as we ate them, and we compared their merits. There was a rivalry among them, and discussion about puff pastry or short pastry.

All these small presents were moving to and fro before Christmas, leading up to the great day, keeping us in a state of excitement, as we prepared for the birthday of the Holy Child. The giving of Christmas-boxes made a bond between all classes of society, we shared the same pleasures, we had the same expectations and joy over simple things.

ALISON UTTLEY
Country Things

On Christmas Presents

A little while ago I saw a statement by Mrs Eddy [Mary Baker Eddy, the founder of Christian Science] on this subject, in which she said that she did not give presents in a gross, sensuous, terrestrial sense, but sat still and thought about Truth and Purity till all her friends were much better for it. Now I do not say that this plan is either superstitious or impossible, and no doubt it has an economic charm. I say it is un-Christian in the same solid and prosaic sense that playing a tune backwards is unmusical or saying 'ain't' is ungrammatical. I do not know that there is any Scriptural text or Church Council that condemns Mrs Eddy's theory of Christmas presents: but Christianity condemns it, as soldiering condemns running away. The two attitudes are antagonistic not only in their theology, not only in their thought, but in their state of soul before they ever begin to think. The idea of embodying goodwill – that is, of putting it into a body – is the huge and primal idea of the Incarnation. A gift of God that can be seen and touched is the whole point of the epigram of the creed. Christ Himself was a Christmas present. The note of material Christmas presents is struck even before He is born in the first movements of the sages and the star. The Three Kings came to Bethlehem bringing gold and frankincense and myrrh. If they had only brought Truth and Purity and Love there would have been no Christian art and no Christian civilisation . . .

G K CHESTERTON
The Theology of Christmas Presents

* * *

Christmas presents are a standing protest on behalf of giving as distinct from that mere sharing that modern moralists offer as equivalent or superior. Christmas stands for this superb and sacred paradox: that it is a higher spiritual transaction for Tommy and Molly each to give each other sixpence than for both equally to share a shilling. Christmas is something better than a thing for all; it is a thing for everybody. And if anyone finds such phrases aimless or fantastic, or thinks that the distinction has no existence except in a refinement of words, the only test is that I have indicated already – the permanent test of the populace. Take any hundred girls from a board school and see whether they do not make a distinction between a flower for each and a garden for all. If therefore new spiritual schools are concerned to prove that they have the spirit and secret of the Christian festival, they must prove it, not by abstract affirmations, but by things that have a special and unmistakable smack, by hitting one pungent tinge of taste, by being able to write a Christmas carol, or even to make a Christmas pie.

G K CHESTERTON
The Contemporary Review, January 1910

Christmas for Animals

Advent preparations are not simply to be confined to our fellow men and women. St Francis of Assisi would often say:

If I were to speak to the Emperor, I would, supplicating and persuading him tell him for the love of God and me to make a special law that no man should take or kill sister Larks, nor do them any harm. Likewise, that all the Podestas of the towns, and the Lords of castles and villages, should be bound every year on Christmas day to compel men to throw wheat and other grains outside the cities and castles, that our sister Larks may have something to eat, and also the other birds, on a day of such solemnity.

And that for the reverence of the Son of God, Who rested on that night with the most blessed Virgin Mary between an Ox and an Ass, they shall be bound to provide for them on that night the best of good fodder. Likewise on that day, all poor men should be satisfied by the rich with good food. For the blessed Father had a greater reverence for Christmas day than for any other festival, saying, 'Since the Lord had been born for us, it behoves us to be saved,' and on account of which he wished that on that day every Christian should rejoice in the Lord; and for His love who gave Himself for us, that all should provide largely not only for the poor, but also for the animals and birds.

The Mirror of Perfection

The Reminder

While I watch the Christmas blaze
Paint the room with ruddy rays,
Something makes my vision glide
To the frosty scene outside.

There, to reach a rotting berry,
Toils a thrush – constrained to very
Dregs of food by sharp distress,
Taking such with thankfulness.

Why, O starving bird, when I
One day's joy would justify,
And put misery out of view,
Do you make me notice you?

THOMAS HARDY

The Crib

They are making a crèche at the Saturday morning classes
For the Christmas party: scissors and paper vie
With fingers and plasticine until there are masses
Of sheep and shepherds that kneel and stand and lie,

And cotton-batting angels with cellophane wings
And a golden cardboard star and string to guide it
And pipe-cleaner camels carrying tin-foil kings
And a real straw manger with Joseph and Mary beside it.

But the manger is empty. The Saturday classes contain
So many different faiths, there is a danger
Of giving offence; there was once no room in the inn,
Now there is no room for him in the manger.

Of course he will understand, his love is hearty
Enough to forgive and forget the being slighted
And true enough not to offend at the birthday party
By showing up where he is uninvited.

Besides he is long accustomed to the manners
Of centuries that consecrate the snub
Of Christmas honoured, not the one it honours.
Strange they should trouble to give the crèche a crib.

ROBERT FINCH

The First Christmas Crib at Greccio

It is an irony that the first crib, made by St Francis to show the villagers at Greccio the shocking, grim realities of birth in a stable, has grown into a familiar, expected institution. From the guildpageants to the Sunday School children's nativity play, and in every medium from wood, china, cardboard to plaster-of-paris, we see the still centre of the Christmas story – the baby Jesus lying in the manger at Bethlehem. Some scholars now believe that Luke's gospel account is poetry – written to teach us something about Christ's birth, but not a historical account of what happened. If we let this shake our faith, we are looking for the wrong assurances. Francis – being both a poet and a mystic – saw straight to the heart of the story. He saw the beauty and helplessness of a human baby set against the squalid conditions of the stable; the presence of the animals, waiting like us for their king; the dramatic contrast between the poverty of the stable and the richness of God's love.

Now three years before his death it befell that he [St Francis] was minded, at the town of Greccio, to celebrate the memory of the Birth of the Child Jesus, with all the added solemnity that he might, for the kindling of devotion. That his might not seem an innovation, he sought and obtained licence from the Supreme Pontiff, and then made ready a manger, and bade hay, together with an ox and an ass, be brought unto the spot. The Brethren were called together, the folk assembled, the wood echoed with their voices, and that august night was made radiant and solemn with many bright lights, and with tuneful and sonorous praises. The man of God, filled with tender love, stood before the manger, bathed in tears, and overflowing with joy. Solemn Masses were celebrated over the manger, Francis, the Levite of Christ, chanting the Holy Gospel. Then he preached unto the folk standing round of the Birth of the King in poverty, calling Him, when he wished to name Him, the Child of Bethlehem, by reason of his tender love for Him.

A certain knight, valorous and true, Messer John of Greccio, who was for the love of Christ had left the secular army, and was bound by closest friendship unto the man of God, declared that he beheld a little Child right fair to see sleeping in that

25

manger, Who seemed to be awakened from sleep when the blessed Father Francis embraced Him in both arms. This vision of the devout knight is rendered worth of belief, not alone through the holiness of him that beheld it, but is also confirmed by the truth that it set forth, and withal proven by the miracles that followed it. For the ensample of Francis, if meditated upon by the world, must needs stir up sluggish hearts unto the faith of Christ, and the hay that was kept back from the manger by the folk proved a marvellous remedy for sick beasts, and a prophylactic against divers other plagues, God magnifying by all means His servant, and making manifest by clear and miraculous portents the efficacy of his powers.

ST BONAVENTURE
The Life of St Francis

A Christmas Letter from Germany

There is a Christmas custom here which pleased and interested me. The children make little presents to their parents, and to each other, and the parents to their children. For three or four months before Christmas the girls are all busy, and the boys save up their pocket money to buy these presents. What the present is to be is cautiously kept secret; and the girls have a world of contrivances to conceal it – such as working when they are out on visits, and the others are not with them, getting up in the morning before daylight, etc. Then on the evening before Christmas Day, one of the parlours is lighted up by the children, into which the parents must not go; a great yew bough is fastened on the table at a little distance from the wall, a multitude of little tapers are fixed in the bough, but not so as to burn it till they are nearly consumed, and coloured paper, etc., hangs and flutters from the twigs. Under this bough the children lay out in great order the presents they mean for their parents, still concealing in the pockets what they intend for each other. Then the parents are introduced, and each presents his little gift; they then bring out the remainder one by one from their pockets, and present them with kisses and embraces. Where I witnessed this scene there were eight or nine children, and the eldest daughter and the mother wept aloud for joy and tenderness; and the tears ran down the face of the father, and he clasped all his children so tight to his breast, it seemed as if he did it to stifle the sob that was rising within it. I was very much affected . . .

SAMUEL TAYLOR COLERIDGE

Waiting for Christmas in Austria

The next day was the big night, Holy Eve, as it is called in Austria. Snow had fallen overnight. We went to church with the older children. The church was filled as on Sunday. Everybody goes to confession on Holy Eve, so one had to wait in line. It was quite early and pitch-dark outside. There were no electric lights in the church, and, of course, it was not heated. The people had brought candles with them, fastened them to the pews, and, holding their hymn-books with heavily-mittened hands close to the little flame, they could read the words of the ancient Advent song, which was softly accompanied by the organ and sung by the whole community: 'Tauet Himmel den Gerechten'. In the flicker of candlelight one could see a neat little frosty cloud in front of every mouth. From under the choir loft, where the confessional stood, one could hear the shuffling of hobnailed boots and also, eventually, the rubbing of hands, the feeble attempts to keep warm when it was below zero outside with yard-long icicles growing from the church roof. But cold belonged to Christmas as heat to the hay-making days. This was as it should be, and nobody gave it a thought.

When Holy Mass was over, we went with the children to the side altar. There in a little wood of spruce trees, was the whole town of Bethlehem spread out before our eyes. The shepherds were already out in the field with their flock. Mary and Joseph had arrived at the cave. They were kneeling beside the manger, which was still empty. Ox and ass, the sheep in the pasture, and the angels in the air seemed to hold their breath, waiting in holy expectation of the little Child to come. Mankind had waited patiently thousands of years for this moment. It couldn't wait any longer; and this is the very feeling you bring home from church yourself in your own heart after a glance into the still-empty manger: you feel you can't wait any longer.

As everything comes to an end in life, so also the long hours of the afternoon passed. Holy Eve is a fast day, and so lunch was over quickly with only one dish, a thick soup. The children spent the day putting their rooms, wardrobes, and drawers in perfect order. In the afternoon we all dressed in our best, and for the last time, we all met under the Advent wreath, all four candles lit. The servants were called in, and once again we sang the old Advent hymn. Before the third verse was over, the silvery sound of a little bell was heard. This was it! The Holy Child had come. Led by the father of the house, the two youngest girls clinging to his hands, we all went down the curved stairway. After a few steps through the wide-open door, we all stopped in a semicircle, gazing in speechless wonder at the Christmas tree, whose solemn beauty dominated the room. The Captain started 'Silent Night'. After we had sung all three verses, there was a moment of complete silence. A fine scent of fir, wax, and *Lebkuchen* lingered in the air. The room was bathed in that mild, golden light which only wax candles can give.

Then the Captain went round wishing everybody a blessed Christmas. The spell was broken.

MARIA VON TRAPP
The Trapp Family Singers

Christmas Eve in India

Sister Honey had spent hours in making a Crib for the children; she had put it inside the porch as there was no room in the chapel, and it was made of spruce and bamboo boughs strangely mingled together. The figures for it had been sent from Canstead too, and she made them change colour by holding strips of coloured talc across a light. She made a rosy Bethlehem dawn outside the Inn, or a strong noon in yellow, or moonlight, shadowing with blue, the tinsel star. The people thought it was wonderful and Sister Honey was gratified by their numbers, but she did not know that Ayah had invited them with promises of a free show and free tea. There were the women in their respectable gowns, the men who were so dirty in comparison and, most of all, the children.

'Why have the devils with wings come to mock at the poor baby?' asked the children, pointing to the angels.

'The baby is the Number One Lord Jesus Christ,' Ayah told them.

'But He hasn't any clothes on! Aren't they going to give Him anything? Not a little red robe? Not a bit of melted butter?'

'This is His Mother,' said Ayah, showing them the little porcelain Virgin in blue and white and pink. 'He is her child.'

'*That* isn't true,' said the women, measuring the baby with their eyes. 'He is too big to be possible. Probably He's a dragon, a bhût in the shape of a child, and presently He'll eat up the woman.'

They were all afraid of bhûts, Hindus and Buddhists alike, and the little Christian Joseph would not go down to Mr Dean's house alone at night because of the bhût who lived on the road.

All day the people came softly in and out; the porch was full of voices respectfully low, and of feet coming and going. A tide of love and liking seemed to lap the Convent; it was in Ayah's dark skirts as she went to welcome them in, and it was in the china figures under the boughs of spruce; it came from the children's happy faces as they crowded round, and was in the nuns' voices as they spoke to one another and in the candles they had lit before the Crib. All day Sister Clodagh had felt that sense of success and love and again she wrote glowingly to Mother Dorothea.

RUMER GODDEN
Black Narcissus

Hospitality for the Homeless

The Traveller comes across an ancient charity inscribed over a little old door as he wanders about the old Cathedral city of Rochester, one Christmas Eve:

RICHARD WATTS, Esq.
by his Will, dated 22 Aug. 1579,
founded this Charity
for Six poor Travellers,
who not being ROGUES, or PROCTORS,
May receive gratis for one Night,
Lodging, Entertainment,
and Fourpence each.

Knowing that he is not a Proctor, and hoping that he is not a Rogue, the Traveller decides to claim his due . . .

I found it to be a clean white house, of a staid and venerable air, with the quaint old door already three times mentioned [an arched door], choice little long low lattice-windows, and a roof of three gables . . . I was very well pleased, both with my property and its situation. While I was yet surveying it with growing content, I espied, at one of the upper lattices which stood open, a decent body, of a wholesome matronly appearance, whose eyes I caught enquiringly addressed to mine. They said so plainly, 'Do you wish to see the houses?' that I answered aloud, 'Yes, if you please.' And within a minute the old door opened, and I bent my head, and went down two steps into the entry.

'This,' said the matronly presence, ushering me into a low room on the right, 'is where the Travellers sit by the fire, and cook what bits of suppers they buy with their fourpences.'

'O! Then they have no Entertainment?' said I. For the inscription over the outer door was still running in my head, and I was mentally repeating, in a kind of tune, 'Lodging, entertainment, and fourpence each.'

'They have a fire provided for 'em,' returned the matron, – a mighty civil person, not, as I could make out, overpaid; 'and these cooking utensils. And this what's painted on a board is the rules for their behaviour. They have their fourpences when

32

they get their tickets from the steward over the way – for I don't admit 'em myself, they must get their tickets first – and sometimes one buys a rasher of bacon, and another a herring, and another a pound of potatoes, or what not. Sometimes two or three of 'em will club their fourpences together, and make a supper that way. But not much of anything is to be got for fourpence, at present, when provisions is so dear.'

'True indeed,' I remarked. I had been looking about the room, admiring its snug fire-side at the upper end, its glimpse of the street through the low mullioned window, and its beams overhead. 'It is very comfortable,' said I.

'Ill-conwenient,' observed the matronly presence.

I liked to hear her say so; for it showed a commendable anxiety to execute in no niggardly spirit the intentions of Master Richard Watts. But the room was really so well adapted to its purpose that I protested, quite enthusiastically, against her disparagement.

'Nay, ma'am,' said I. 'I am sure it is warm in winter and cool in summer. It has a look of homely welcome and soothing rest. It has a remarkably cosy fireside, the very blink of which, gleaming out into the street upon a winter night, is enough to warm all Rochester's heart. And as to the convenience of the six Poor Travellers – '

'I don't mean them,' returned the presence. 'I speak of its being an ill-conwenience to myself and my daughter, having no other room to sit in of a night.'

This was true enough, but there was another quaint room of corresponding dimensions on the opposite side of the entry: so I stepped across to it, through the open doors of both rooms, and asked what this chamber was for.

'This,' returned the presence, 'is the Board Room. Where the gentlemen meet when they come here.'

Let me see. I had counted from the street six upper windows besides these on the ground-story. Making a perplexed calculation in my mind, I rejoined, 'Then the six Poor Travellers sleep up-stairs?'

My new friend shook her head. 'They sleep,' she answered, 'in two little outer galleries at the back, where their beds has always been, ever since the Charity was founded. It being so very ill-conwenient to me as things is at present, the gentlemen are going to take off a bit of the back-yard, and make a slip of a room for 'em three, to sit in before they go to bed.'

'And then the six Poor Travellers,' said I, 'will be entirely out of the house?'

'Entirely out of the house,' assented the presence, comfortably smoothing her hands. 'Which is considered much better for all parties, and much more conwenient.'

I had been a little startled, in the Cathedral, by the emphasis with which the effigy of Master Richard Watts was bursting out of his tomb; but I began to think, now, that it might be expected to come across the High-street some stormy night, and make a disturbance here.

* * *

'And pray, ma'am,' said I, sensible that the blankness of my face began to brighten as the thought occurred to me, 'could one see these Travellers?'

'Well!' she returned dubiously, 'no!'

'Not tonight, for instance?' said I.

'Well!' she returned more positively, 'no. Nobody ever asked to see them, and nobody ever did see them.'

As I am not easily balked in a design when I am set upon it, I urged to the good lady that this was Christmas Eve; that Christmas comes but once a year – which is unhappily too true, for when it begins to stay with us the whole year round we shall make this earth a very different place; that I was possessed by the desire to treat the Travellers to a supper and a temperate glass of hot Wassail; that the voice of Fame had been heard in that land, declaring my ability to make hot Wassail; that if I were permitted to hold the feast, I should be found conformable to reason, sobriety, and good hours; in a word, that I could be merry and wise myself, and had been even known at a pinch to keep others so, although I was decorated with no badge or medal, and was not a Brother, Orator, Apostle, Saint, or Prophet of any denomination whatever. In the end I prevailed, to my great joy. It was settled that at nine o'clock that night a Turkey and a piece of Roast Beef should smoke upon the board; and that I, faint and unworthy minister for once of Master Richard Watts, should preside as the Christmas-supper host of the six Poor Travellers.

I went back to my inn to give the necessary directions for the

Turkey and Roast Beef, and, during the remainder of the day, could settle to nothing for thinking of the Poor Travellers. When the wind blew hard against the windows, – it was a cold day, with dark gusts of sleet alternating with periods of wild brightness, as if the year were dying fitfully, – I pictured them advancing towards their resting-place along various cold roads, and felt delighted to think how little they foresaw the supper that awaited them. I painted their portraits in my mind, and indulged in little heightening touches. I made them footsore; I made them weary; I made them carry packs and bundles; I made them stop by finger-posts and milestones, leaning on their bent sticks, and looking wistfully at what was written there; I made them lose their way; and filled their five wits with apprehensions of lying out all night, and being frozen to death. I took up my hat, and went out, climbed to the top of the Old Castle, and looked over the windy hills that slope down to the Medway, almost believing that I could descry some of my Travellers in the distance. After it fell dark, and the Cathedral bell was heard in the invisible steeple – quite a bower of frosty rime when I had last seen it – striking five, six, seven, I became so full of my Travellers that I could eat no dinner, and felt constrained to watch them still in the red coals of my fire.

* * *

The Travellers were all assembled, the cloth was laid . . . I found the party to be thus composed. Firstly, myself. Secondly, a very decent man indeed, with his right arm in a sling, who had a certain clean agreeable smell of wood about him, from which I judged him to have something to do with shipbuilding. Thirdly, a little sailor-boy, a mere child, with a profusion of rich dark brown hair, and deep womanly-looking eyes. Fourthly, a shabby-genteel personage in a threadbare black suit, and apparently in very bad circumstances, with a dry suspicious look; the absent buttons on his waistcoat eked out with red tape; and a bundle of extraordinarily tattered papers sticking out of an inner breast-pocket. Fifthly, a foreigner by birth, but an Englishman in speech, who carried his pipe in the band of his hat, and lost no time in telling me, in an easy, simple, engaging way, that he was a watchmaker from Geneva, and travelled all about the Continent, mostly on foot, working as a journeyman, and seeing new countries, – possibly (I thought) also smuggling a watch or so, now and then. Sixthly, a little widow, who had been very pretty and was still very young, but whose beauty had been wrecked in some great misfortune, and whose manner was remarkably timid, scared, and solitary. Seventhly and lastly, a Traveller of a kind familiar to my boyhood, but now almost obsolete, – a Book-Pedler, who had a quantity of Pamphlets and Numbers with him, and who presently boasted that he could repeat more verses in an evening than he could sell in a twelvemonth ... It made my heart rejoice to observe how their wind and frost hardened faces softened in the clatter of plates and knives and forks, and mellowed in the fire and supper heat. While their hats and caps and wrappers, hanging up, a few small bundles on the ground in a corner, and in another corner three or four old walking sticks, worn down at the end to a mere fringe, linked this snug interior with the bleak outside in a golden chain.

CHARLES DICKENS
Christmas Stories

Noblesse Oblige

Sara Crewe, the fabulously rich 'little princess' has been orphaned and abandoned to the cruel mercies of Mrs Minchin. Living in the same square is a large, happy family whom Sara secretly watches with longing and affection, giving them romantic names and stories.

One evening a very funny thing happened – though, perhaps, in one sense it was not a funny thing at all.

Several of the Montmorencys were evidently going to a children's party, and just as Sara was about to pass the door they were crossing the pavement to get into the carriage which was waiting for them. Veronica Eustacia and Rosalind Gladys, in white lace frocks and lovely sashes, had just got in, and Guy Clarence, aged five, was following them. He was such a pretty fellow and had such a darling little round head covered with curls, that Sara forgot her basket and shabby cloak altogether – in fact, forgot everything but that she wanted to look at him for a moment. So she paused and looked.

It was Christmas time, and the Large Family had been hearing many stories about children who were poor and had no mammas and papas to fill their stockings and take them to the pantomime – children who were, in fact, cold and thinly clad and hungry. In the stories, kind people – sometimes little boys and girls with tender hearts – invariably saw the poor children and gave them money or rich gifts, or took them home to beautiful dinners. Guy Clarence had been affected to tears that very afternoon by the reading of such a story, and he had burned with desire to find such a poor child and give her a certain sixpence he possessed, and thus provide for her for life. An entire sixpence, he was sure, would mean affluence for evermore. As he crossed the strip of red carpet laid across the pavement from the door to the carriage, he had this very sixpence in the pocket of his very short man-o'-war trousers. And just as Rosalind Gladys got into the vehicle and jumped on to the seat in order to feel the cushions spring under her, he saw Sara standing on the wet pavement in her shabby frock and hat, with her old basket on her arm, looking at him hungrily.

He thought that her eyes looked hungry because she perhaps

had nothing to eat for a long time. He did not know that they looked so because she was hungry for the warm, merry life his home held and his rosy face spoke of, and that she had a hungry wish to snatch him in her arms and kiss him. He only knew that she had big eyes and a thin face and thin legs, and a common basket and poor clothes. So he put his hand in his pocket and found his sixpence, and walked up to her benignly.

'Here, poor little girl,' he said. 'Here is a sixpence. I will give it to you.'

Sara started, and all at once realized that she looked exactly like poor children she had seen, in her better days, waiting on the pavement to watch her as she got out of her brougham. And she had given them pennies many a time. Her face went red and then it went pale, and for a second she felt as if she could not take the dear little sixpence.

'Oh, no!' she said. 'Oh no, thank you; I mustn't take it, indeed!'

Her voice was so unlike an ordinary street child's voice, and her manner was so like the manner of a well-bred little person that Veronica Eustacia (whose real name was Janet) and Rosalind Gladys (who was really called Nora) leaned forward to listen.

But Guy Clarence was not to be thwarted in his benevolence. He thrust the sixpence into her hand.

'Yes, you must take it, poor girl!' he insisted stoutly. 'You can buy things to eat with it. It is a whole sixpence!'

There was something so honest and kind in his face, and he looked so likely to be heartbrokenly disappointed if she did not take it, that Sara knew that she must not refuse him. To be as proud as that would be a cruel thing. So she actually put her pride in her pocket, though it must be admitted her cheeks burned.

'Thank you,' she said. 'You are a kind, kind little darling thing.' And as he scrambled joyfully into the carriage she went away, trying to smile, though she caught her breath quickly and her eyes were shining through a mist. She had known that she looked odd and shabby, but until now she had not known that she might be taken for a beggar.

FRANCES HODGSON BURNETT
A Little Princess

Christmas Day in the Workhouse

It is Christmas Day in the Workhouse,
   And the cold bare walls are bright
With garlands of green and holly,
   And the place is a pleasant sight:
For with clean-washed hands and faces,
   In a long and hungry line
The paupers sit at the tables,
   For this is the hour they dine.

And the guardians and their ladies,
   Although the wind is east,
Have come in their furs and wrappers,
   To watch their charges feast;
To smile and be condescending,
   Put pudding on pauper plates,
To be hosts at the workhouse banquet
   They've paid for – with the rates.

Oh, the paupers are meek and lowly
   With their 'Thank'ee kindly, mum's';
So long as they fill their stomachs,
   What matter it whence it comes?
But one of the old men mutters,
   And pushes his plate aside:
'Great God!' he cries; 'but it chokes me!
   For this is the day *she* dies.'

The guardians gazed in horror;
   The master's face went white;
'Did a pauper refuse their pudding?'
   'Could their eyes believe aright?'
Then the ladies clutched their husbands,
   Thinking the man would die,
Struck by a bolt, or something,
   By the outraged One on high.

But the pauper sat for a moment,
   Then rose 'mid a silence grim.

For the others had ceased to chatter,
    And trembled in every limb.
He looked at the guardians' ladies,
    Then, eyeing their lords, he said,
'I eat not the food of villains
    Whose hands are foul and red:

'Whose victims cry for vengeance
    From their dank, unhallowed graves.'
'He's drunk!' said the workhouse master,
    'Or else he's mad, and raves.'
'Not drunk, or mad,' cried the pauper,
    'But only a haunted beast,
Who, torn by the hounds and mangled,
    Declines and vulture's feast.

'I care not a curse for the guardians,
    And I won't be dragged away.
Just let me have the fit out.
    'It's only on Christmas Day
That the black past comes to goad me,
    And prey on my burning brain;
I'll tell you the rest in a whisper, –
    I swear I won't shout again.

'Keep your hands off me, curse you!
    Hear me right out to the end.
You come here to see how the paupers
    The season of Christmas spend.
You come here to watch us feeding,
    As they watch the captured beast.
Hear why a penniless pauper
    Spits on your paltry feast.

'Do you think I will take your bounty,
    And let you smile and think
You're doing a noble action
    With the parish's meat and drink?
Where is my wife, you traitors –
    The poor old wife you slew?

Yes, by the God above us,
  My Nance was killed by you!

'Last winter my wife lay dying,
  Starved in a filthy den;
I had never been to the parish, –
  I came to the parish then.
I swallowed my pride in coming,
  For, ere the ruin came,
I held up my head as a trader,
  And I bore a spotless name.

'I came to the parish, craving
  Bread for a starving wife,
Bread for the woman who'd loved me
  Through fifty years of life;
And what do you think they told me,
  Mocking my awful grief?
That "the House" was open to us,
  But they wouldn't give "out relief".

'I slunk to the filthy alley –
  'Twas a cold, raw Christmas eve –
And the bakers' shops were open,
  Tempting a man to thieve;
But I clenched my fists together,
  Holding my head awry,
So I came to her empty-handed,
  And mournfully told her why.

Then I told her, "the House" was open;
  She had heard of the ways of *that*,
For her bloodless cheeks went crimson,
  And up in her rags she sat,
Crying, "Bide the Christmas here, John,
  We've never had one apart;
I think I can bear the hunger, –
  The other would break my heart."

'All through that eve I watched her,
  Holding her hand in mine,

Praying the Lord, and weeping
  Till my lips were salt as brine,
I asked her once if she hungered,
  And as she answered "No,"
The moon shone in at the window
  Set in a wreath of snow.

'Then the room was bathed in glory,
  And I saw in my darling's eyes
The far-away look of wonder
  That comes when the spirit flies;
And her lips were parched and parted,
  And her reason came and went,
For she raved of our home in Devon,
  Where our happiest years were spent.

'And the accents, long forgotten,
  Came back to the tongue once more,
For she talked like the country lassie
  I woo'd by the Devon shore,
Then she rose to her feet and trembled,
  And fell on the rags and moaned,
And, "Give me a crust – I'm famished –
  For the love of God!" she groaned.

'I rushed from the room like a madman,
  And flew to the workhouse gate.
Crying, "Food for a dying woman!"
  And the answer came, "Too late."
They drove me away with curses;
  Then I fought with a dog in the street,
And tore from the mongrel's clutches
  A crust he was trying to eat.

'Back, through the filthy by-lanes!
  Back, through the trampled slush!
Up to the crazy garret,
  Wrapped in an awful hush.
My heart sank down at the threshold,
  And I paused with a sudden thrill,

For there in the silv'ry moonlight
    My Nance lay, cold and still.

'Up to the blackened ceiling
    The sunken eyes were cast –
I knew on those lips all bloodless
    My name had been the last;
She'd called for her absent husband –
    O God! had I but known! –
Had called in vain, and in anguish
    Had died in that den – *alone*.

'Yes, there, in a land of plenty,
    Lay a loving woman dead,
Cruelly starved and murdered
    For a loaf of the parish bread.
At yonder gate, last Christmas,
    I craved for a human life.
You, who would feast us paupers,
    What of my murdered wife!

'There, get ye gone to your dinners;
    Don't mind me in the least;
Think of the happy paupers
    Eating your Christmas feast;
And when you recount their blessings
    In your smug parochial way,
Say what you did for *me*, too,
    Only last Christmas Day.'

GEORGE SIMS

The House of Christmas

There fared a mother driven forth,
Out of an inn to roam;
In the place where she was homeless
All men are at home.
The crazy stable close at hand,
With shaking timber and shifting sand,
Grew a stronger thing to abide and stand
Than the square stones of Rome.

For men are homesick in their homes,
And strangers under the sun,
And they lay their heads in a foreign land
Whenever the day is done.
Here we have battle and blazing eyes
And chance and honour and high surprise,
But our homes are under miraculous skies
Where the yule tale was begun.

A child in a foul stable,
Where the beasts feed and foam;
Only where he was homeless
Are you and I at home;
We have hands that fashion and heads that know,
But our hearts we lost – how long ago!
In a place no chart nor ship can show
Under the sky's dome.

This world is wild as an old wives' tale,
And strange the plain things are,
The earth is enough and the air is enough
For our wonder and our war;
But our rest is as far as the fire-drake swings
And our peace is put in impossible things
Where clashed and thundered unthinkable wings
Round an incredible star.

To an open house in the evening
Home shall all men come,
To an older place than Eden
And a taller town than Rome.
To the end of the way of the wandering star,
To the things that cannot be and that are,
To the place where God was homeless
And all men are at home.

G K CHESTERTON

2

Nativity

The King is Coming

Yet if His Majesty, our sovereign Lord,
Should of his own accord
Friendly himself invite,
And say 'I'll be your guest to-morrow night,'
How should we stir ourselves, call and command
All hands to work! 'Let no man idle stand!
'Set me fine Spanish tables in the hall;
See they be fitted all;
Let there be room to eat
And order taken that there want no meat.
See every sconce and candlestick made bright,
That without tapers they may give a light.
'Look to the presence; are the carpets spread,
The dazie o'er the head,
The cushions in the chairs,
And all the candles lighted on the stairs?
Perfume the chambers, and in any case
Let each man give attendance in his place!'
Thus, if a king were coming, would we do;
And 'twere good reason too;
For 'tis a duteous thing
To show all honour to an earthly king,
And after all our travail and our cost
So he be pleased, to think no labour lost.

But at the coming of the King of Heaven
All's set at six and seven;
We wallow in our sin,
Christ cannot find a chamber in the inn.
We entertain Him always like a stranger,
And, as at first, still lodge Him in the manger.

ANONYMOUS

Christmas

All after pleasures as I rode one day,
   My horse and I, both tired, body and mind,
With full cry of affections, quite astray,
   I took up in the next inn I could find.

There when I came, whom found I but my dear,
   My dearest Lord, expecting till the grief
Of pleasures brought me to Him, ready there
   To be all passengers' sweet relief.

O Thou, Whose glorious yet contracted light,
   Wrapped in Night's mantle, stole into a manger,
Since my dark soul and brutish, is Thy right,
   To man, of all beasts, be not Thou a stranger:

Furnish and deck my soul, that Thou mayst have
A better lodging than a rack or grave.

GEORGE HERBERT

No Room

No room at the Holiday Inn;
No room in the holiday for them!
'Two hots and a cot' at the 'Army'
And a cardboard box
   over a sewer grate
   Is 'home' and a 'central heat'.

And they shall be called
   'shopping bag ladies',
   'street people',
   'the homeless'.

They know about
   giving birth on the run
   and keeping on the move
     to stay alive.
Smelly places of birth
   and lonely places of death
   are more than
     Bible stories to them.

They peer into the window
   of my soul;
   decorated as it is
   with Christmas lights
   and presents under the tree.
And I gaze out into the dark:
   the night in which
   an anonymous Joseph and Mary
   seek a place in my world
   for love to be born.

No room in the Holiday Inn;
   not even room in the holiday
   for love to be born. Alas!

CORNELIUS KANHAI

The Carol Singers of Mellstock

The older men and musicians wore thick coats, with stiff perpendicular collars, and coloured handkerchiefs wound round and round the neck till the end came to hand, over all which they just showed their ears and noses, like people looking over a wall. The remainder, stalwart ruddy men and boys, were dressed mainly in snow-white smock-frocks, embroidered upon the shoulders and breasts in ornamental forms of hearts, diamonds, and zigzags. The cider-mug was emptied for the ninth time, the music-books were arranged, and the pieces finally decided upon. The boys in the meantime put the old horn-lanterns in order, cut candles into short lengths to fit the lanterns; and, a thin fleece of snow having fallen since the early part of the evening, those who had no leggings went to the stable and wound wisps of hay round their ankles to keep the insidious flakes from the interior of their boots . . .

Just before the clock struck twelve they lighted the lanterns and started. The moon, in her third quarter, had risen since the snow-storm; but the dense accumulation of snow-cloud weakened her power to a faint twilight which was rather pervasive of the landscape than traceable to the sky. The breeze had gone down, and the rustle of their feet and tones of their speech echoed with an alert rebound from every post, boundary-stone, and ancient wall they passed, even where the distance of the echo's origin was less than a few yards. Beyond their own slight noises nothing was to be heard save the occasional bark of foxes in the direction of Yalbury Wood, or the brush of a rabbit among the grass now and then as it scampered out of their way.

Most of the outlying homesteads and hamlets had been visited by about two o'clock; they then passed across the outskirts of a wooded part toward the main village, nobody being at home at the Manor. Pursuing no recognized track, great care was necessary in walking lest their faces should come in contact with the low-hanging boughs of the old lime-trees, which in many spots formed dense overgrowths of interlaced branches . . .

By this time they were crossing to a gate in the direction of the school which, standing on a slight eminence at the junction of three ways, now rose in unvarying and dark flatness against the sky. The instruments were retuned, and all the band entered the school enclosure, enjoined by old William to keep upon the grass.

'Number seventy-eight,' he softly gave out as they formed round in a semicircle, the boys opening the lanterns to get a clearer light, and directing their rays on the books.

Then passed forth into the quiet night an ancient and time-worn hymn, embodying a quaint Christianity in words orally transmitted from father to son through several generations down to the present characters, who sang them out right earnestly:

> *Remember Adam's fall,*
> *O thou Man:*
> *Remember Adam's fall*
> *From Heaven to Hell.*
> *Remember Adam's fall;*
> *How he hath condemn'd all*
> *In Hell perpetual*
> *There for to dwell . . .*

Having concluded the last note they listened for a minute or two, but found that no sound issued from the schoolhouse.

'Four breaths, and then, "O, what unbounded goodness!", number fifty-nine,' said William.

This was duly gone through, and no notice whatever seemed to be taken of the performance.

'Good guide us, surely 'tisn't a' empty house, as befell us in the year thirty-nine and forty-three!' said old Dewy.

'Perhaps she's jist come from some musical city, and sneers at our doings?' the tranter whispered.

''Od rabbit her!' said Mr Penny, with an annihilating look at a corner of the school chimney, 'I don't quite stomach her, if this is it. Your plain music well done is as worthy as your other sort done bad, a' b'lieve, souls; so say I.'

'Four breaths, and then the last,' said the leader authoritatively. '"Rejoice, ye Tenants of the Earth", number sixty-four.'

At the close, waiting yet another minute, he said in a clear loud voice, as he said in the village at that hour and season for the previous forty years –

'A merry Christmas to ye!'

* * *

Farmer Shiner's was a queer lump of a house, standing at the corner of a lane that ran into the principal thoroughfare. The upper windows were much wider than they were high, and this feature, together with a broad bay-window where the door might have been expected, gave it by day the aspect of a human countenance turned askance, and wearing a sly and wicked leer. Tonight nothing was visible but the outline of the roof upon the sky.

The front of this building was reached, and the preliminaries arranged as usual.

'Four breaths, and number thirty-two, "Behold the Morning Star"', said old William.

They had reached the end of the second verse, and the fiddlers were doing the up-bow stroke previously to pouring forth the opening chord of the third verse, when, without a light appearing or any signal being given a roaring voice exclaimed –

'Shut up, woll 'ee! Don't make your blaring row here! A feller wi' a headache enough to split his skull likes a quiet night!'

Slam went the window.

'Hullo, that's a' ugly blow for we!' said the tranter, in a keenly appreciative voice, and turning to his companions.

'Finish the carrel, all who be friends of harmony!' commanded old William; and they continued to the end.

'Four breaths, and number nineteen!' said William firmly. 'Give it him well; the quire can't be insulted in this manner!'

A light now flashed into existence, the window opened, and the farmer stood revealed as one in a terrific passion.

'Drown en! – drown en!' the tranter cried, fiddling frantically. 'Play fortissimy, and drown his spaking!'

'Fortissimy!' said Michael Mail, and the music and singing waxed so loud that it was impossible to know what Mr Shiner had said, was saying, or was about to say; but wildly flinging his arms and body about in the forms of capital Xs and Ys, he appeared to utter enough invectives to consign the whole parish to perdition.

'Very onseemly – very!' said old William, as they retired. 'Never such a dreadful scene in the whole round o' my carrel practice – never! And he a churchwarden!'

'Only a drap o' drink got into his head,' said the tranter. 'Man's well enough when he's in his religious frame. He's in his worldly frame now. Must ask en to our bit of a party to-morrow

54

night, I suppose, and so put en in humour again. We bear no mortal man ill-will.'

THOMAS HARDY
Under the Greenwood Tree

Carollers at Mole End

It was a pretty sight, and a seasonable one, that met their eyes when they flung the door open. In the fore-court, lit by the dim rays of a horn lantern, some eight or ten little field mice stood in a semicircle, red worsted comforters round their throats, their fore-paws thrust deep into their pockets, their feet jigging for warmth. With bright beady eyes they glanced shyly at each other, sniggering a little, sniffing and applying coat-sleeves a good deal. As the door opened, one of the elder ones that carried the lantern was just saying, 'Now then, one, two, three!' and forthwith their shrill little voices uprose on the air, singing one of the old-time carols that their forefathers composed in fields that were fallow and held by frost, or when snow-bound in chimney corners, and handed down to be sung in the miry street to lamp-lit windows at Yuletime.

CAROL

Villagers all, this frosty tide,
Let your doors swing open wide,
Though wind may follow, and snow beside,
Yet draw us in by your fire to bide;
    Joy shall be yours in the morning!

Here we stand in the cold and the sleet,
Blowing fingers and stamping feet,
Come from far away you to greet –
You by the fire and we in the street –
    Bidding you joy in the morning!

For ere one half of the night was gone,
Sudden a star has led us on,
Raining bliss and benison –
Bliss to-morrow and more anon,
    Joy for every morning!

Goodman Joseph toiled through the snow –
Saw the star o'er a stable low;
Mary she might not further go –
Welcome thatch, and litter below!
  Joy was hers in the morning!

And then they heard the angels tell
'Who were the first to cry Nowell?
Animals all, as it befell,
In the stable where they did dwell!
  Joy shall be theirs in the morning!'

The voices ceased, the singers, bashful but smiling, exchanged sidelong glances, and silence succeeded – but for a moment only. Then, from up above and far away, down the tunnel they had so lately travelled was borne to their ears in a faint musical hum the sound of distant bells ringing a joyous and clangerous peal.

'Very well sung, boys!' cried the Rat heartily. 'And now come along in, all of you, and warm yourselves by the fire, and have something hot!'

KENNETH GRAHAME
The Wind in the Willows

The Oxen

Christmas Eve, and twelve of the clock,
  'Now they are all on their knees',
An elder said as we sat in a flock
  By the embers in hearthside ease.

We pictured the meek mild creatures where
  They dwelt in their strawy pen,
Nor did it occur to one of us there
  To doubt they were kneeling then.

So fair a fancy few would weave
  In these years! Yet, I feel,
If some one said on Christmas Eve,
  'Come; see the oxen kneel

'In the lonely barton by yonder coomb
  Our childhood used to know',
I should go with him in the gloom,
  Hoping it might be so.

THOMAS HARDY

Noel: Christmas Eve, 1913
Pax hominibus bonae voluntatis

A frosty Christmas Eve
  When the stars were shining
Fared I forth alone
  where westwards falls this hill,
And from many a village
  in the water's valley
Distant music reach'd me
  peals of bells aringing;
The constellated sounds
  ran sprinkling on earth's floor
As the dark vault above
  with stars spangled o'er.
Then sped my thought to keep
  that first Christmas of all
When the shepherds watching
  by their folds ere the dawn
Heard music in the fields
  and marvelling could not tell
Whether it were angels
  or the bright stars singing.
Now blessed be the tow'rs
  that crown England so fair
That stand up strong in prayer
  unto God for our souls:
Blessed be their founders
  (said I) an' our country folk
Who are ringing for Christ
  in the belfries tonight
With arms lifted to clutch
  the rattling ropes that race
Into the dark above
  and the mad romping din.
But to me afar
  it was starry music
Angel's song, comforting
  as the comfort of Christ

When he spake tenderly
    to his sorrowful flock:
The old words came to me
    by the riches of time
Mellow'd and transfigured
    as I stood on the hill
Heark'ning in the aspect
    of th'eternal silence.

ROBERT BRIDGES

Moonless darkness stands between

Moonless darkness stands between.
Past, O Past, no more be seen!
But the Bethlehem star may lead me
To the sight of Him who freed me
From the self that I have been.
Make me pure, Lord: Thou art holy:
Make me meek, Lord: Thou wert lowly;
Now beginning, and alway:
Now begin, on Christmas day.

GERARD MANLEY HOPKINS

Welcome!

Welcome, all wonders in one sight!
   Eternity shut in a span!
Summer in winter! day in night!
   Heaven in earth! and God in man!
Great little One, whose all-embracing birth,
Lifts earth to heaven, stoops heaven to earth.

RICHARD CRASHAW

The Heavenly Light

The Incarnation did not alter anything, it only revealed the love of God. One night, so to speak, a heavenly light was switched on to earth and men *saw* a baby Face, and *that* was God.

FATHER ANDREW
The Melody of Life

Chanticleer's Carol

All this night shrill chanticleer,
Day's proclaiming trumpeter,
　Claps his wings and loudly cries,
　Mortals, mortals, wake and rise!
　　See a wonder
　　Heaven is under;
　From the earth is risen a Sun
　Shines all night, though day be done.

Wake, O earth, wake everything!
Wake and hear the joy I bring;
　Wake and joy; for all this night
　Heaven and every twinkling light,
　　All amazing
　　Still stand gazing.
　Angels, Powers, and all that be,
　Wake, and joy this Sun to see.

Hail, O Sun, O blessed Light,
Sent into the world by night!
　Let thy rays and heavenly powers
　Shine in these dark souls of ours;
　　For most duly
　　Thou art truly
　God and man, we do confess:
　Hail, O Sun of Righteousness!

WILLIAM AUSTIN

New Prince, New Pomp

Behold a silly tender babe
  In freezing winter night
In homely manger trembling lies:
  Alas! a piteous sight.

The inns are full; no man will yield
  This little pilgrim bed;
But forced he is with silly beasts
  In crib to shroud his head.

Despise not him for lying there;
  First what he is inquire:
An orient pearl is often found
  In depth of dirty mire.

Weigh not his crib, his wooden dish,
  Nor beasts that by him feed;
Weigh not his mother's poor attire,
  Nor Joseph's simple weed.

This stable is a Prince's court,
  This crib his chair of state,
The beasts are parcel of his pomp,
  The wooden dish his plate.

The persons in that poor attire
  His royal liveries wear;
The Prince himself is come from heaven.
  This pomp is prizèd there.

With joy approach, O Christian wight,
  Do homage to thy King;
And highly praise this humble pomp
  Which he from heaven doth bring.

ROBERT SOUTHWELL

Et Incarnatus Est

Love is the plant of peace and most precious of virtues;
For heaven hold it ne might so heavy it seemed,
Till it had on earth yoten himself.
Was never leaf upon linden lighter thereafter,
As when it had of the fold flesh and blood taken;
Then was it portative and piercing as the point of a needle.
May no armour it let, neither high walls.
For-thy is love leader of our Lord's folk of heaven.

WILLIAM LANGLAND

yoten: poured out; *fold*: earth; *For-thy*: therefore

Prayer

Lord, I will go to Mary and make covenant with her, to keep her child, not for her need but for mine. And take to me the sweet child and swathe Him in his cradle with love bands. Lord, help me to put from me the cradle of self love and draw to me the cradle of true love, for that liketh this child to rest Him in, and so in my soul sing lovelike and say:

Lovely little child, fairest of hue,
Have mercy on me, sweet Jesu.

And while I thus sing I will be sorry and think how oft I have received my God and laid Him in a foul common stable to all the seven deadly sins ... and seldom fully cleansed to God's liking; therefore oft sigh and sorrow and shrive me to God as I rock the cradle, and sing and say: Lovely little Child.

ANONYMOUS

Balulalow

O my dear heart, young Jesus sweet,
Prepare thy cradle in my spreit,
And I sall rock thee in my heart,
And never mair from thee depart.

But I sall praise thee evermore,
With sangis sweet unto thy gloir;
The knees of my heart shall I bow,
And sing that richt *Balulalow*.

THE BROTHERS WEDDERBURN

spreit: spirit; *sall*: shall; *sangis*: songs; *gloir*: glory

I only knew he named my name

This excerpt from a very long poem gives the resolution to Browning's struggle between faith in its traditional form and intellectual and religious integrity – a struggle which increases in intensity for us. He is 'woolgathering' during a foolish sermon in an unaccustomed chapel on Christmas Eve . . .

. . . While I watched my foolish heart expand
In the lazy glow of benevolence,
   O'er the various modes of man's belief.
I sprang up with fear's vehemence.
   Needs must there be one way, our chief
Best way of worship: let me strive
To find it, and when found, contrive
My fellows also take their share!
This constitutes my earthly care:
God's is above and distinct.
For I, a man, with men am linked
And not a brute with brutes; no gain
That I experience, must remain
Unshared: but should my best endeavour
To share it, fail – subsisteth ever
God's care above, and I exult
That God, by God's own ways occult,
May – doth, I will believe – bring back
All wanderers to a single track.
Meantime, I can but testify
God's care for me – no more, can I –
It is but for myself I know;
   The world rolls witnessing around me
   Only to leave me as it found me;
Men cry there, but my ear is slow;
Their races flourish or decay
– What boots it, while yon lucid way
Loaded with stars divides the vault?
But soon my soul repairs its fault
When, sharpening sense's hebetude,
She turns on my own life! So viewed,
No mere mote's-breadth but teems immense

With witnessings of providence:
And woe to me if when I look
Upon that record, the sole book
Unsealed to me, I take no heed
Of any warning that I read!
Have I been sure, this Christmas-Eve,
God's own hand did the rainbow weave,
Whereby the truth from heaven slid
Into my soul? – I cannot bid
The world admit he stooped to heal
My soul, as if in a thunder-peal
Where one heard noise, and one saw flame,
I only knew he named my name . . .

ROBERT BROWNING
Christmas Eve and Easter Day

Christmas Present

I make no apology for including this snatch of A Christmas Carol. *For its sheer exuberance there is nothing to beat it – a model for all our New Year's resolutions. Scrooge wakes on Christmas morning from a vision of his loveless life and his future unmourned death.*

Yes! and the bedpost was his own. The bed was his own, the room was his own. Best and happiest of all, the Time before him was his own, to make amends in!

'I will live in the Past, the Present, and the Future!' Scrooge repeated, as he scrambled out of bed. 'The Spirits of all Three shall strive within me. Oh Jacob Marley! Heaven, and the Christmas Time be praised for this! I say it on my knees, old Jacob, on my knees!'

He was so fluttered and so glowing with his good intentions, that his broken voice would scarcely answer to his call. He had been sobbing violently in his conflict with the Spirit, and his face was wet with tears.

'They are not torn down,' cried Scrooge, folding one of his bed-curtains in his arms, 'they are not torn down, rings and all. They are here: I am here: the shadows of the things that would have been may be dispelled. They will be, I know they will!'

His hands were busy with his garments all this time: turning them inside out, putting them on upside down, tearing them, mislaying them, making them parties to every kind of extravagance.

'I don't know what to do!' cried Scrooge, laughing and crying in the same breath; and making a perfect Laocoön of himself with his stockings. 'I am as light as a feather, I am as happy as an angel, I am as merry as a schoolboy. I am as giddy as a drunken man. A Merry Christmas to everybody! A Happy New Year to all the world. Hallo there! Whoop! Hallo!'

He had frisked into the sitting-room, and was now standing there: perfectly winded.

'There's the saucepan that the gruel was in!' cried Scrooge, starting off again, and frisking round the fireplace. 'There's the door, by which the Ghost of Jacob Marley entered! There's the corner where the Ghost of Christmas Present sat! There's the window where I saw the wandering Spirits! It's all right, it's all true, it all happened. Ha, ha, ha!'

Really, for a man who had been out of practice for so many years, it was a splendid laugh, a most illustrious laugh. The father of a long, long line of brilliant laughs!

'I don't know what day of the month it is!' said Scrooge. 'I don't know how long I've been among the Spirits. I don't know anything. I'm quite a baby. Never mind. I don't care. I'd rather be a baby. Hallo! Whoop! Hallo there!' He was checked in his transports by the churches ringing out the lustiest peals he had ever heard. Clash, clang, hammer, ding, dong, bell. Bell, dong, ding, hammer, clang, clash! Oh, glorious, glorious!

Running to the window, he opened it, and put out his head. No fog, no mist; clear, bright, jovial, stirring, cold; cold, piping for the blood to dance to; golden sunlight; heavenly sky; sweet fresh air; merry bells. Oh glorious. Glorious!

'What's today?' cried Scrooge, calling downward to a boy in Sunday clothes, who perhaps had loitered in to look about him.

'EH?' returned the boy, with all his might of wonder.

'What's today, my fine fellow?' said Scrooge.

'Today!' replied the boy. 'Why, CHRISTMAS DAY.'

* * *

He dressed himself 'all in his best', and at last got out into the streets. The people were by this time pouring forth, as he had seen them with the Ghost of Christmas Present; and walking with his hands behind him, Scrooge regarded everyone with a delighted smile. He looked so irresistibly pleasant, in a word, that three or four good-humoured fellows said, 'Good morning, Sir! A Merry Christmas to you!' And Scrooge said often afterwards, that of all the blithe sounds he had ever heard, those were the blithest in his ears.

He had not gone far, when coming on towards him he beheld the portly gentleman, who had walked into his counting-house the day before and said, 'Scrooge and Marley's, I believe?'. It sent a pang across his heart to think how this old gentleman would look upon him when they met; but he knew what path lay straight before him, and he took it.

'My dear Sir,' said Scrooge, quickening his pace, and taking the old gentleman by both his hands. 'How do you do? I hope you succeeded yesterday. It was very kind of you. A Merry Christmas to you, Sir!'

'Mr. Scrooge?'

'Yes,' said Scrooge. 'That is my name, and I fear it may not be pleasant to you. Allow me to ask your pardon. And will you have the goodness' – here Scrooge whispered in his ear.

'Lord bless me!' cried the gentleman, as if his breath were gone. 'My dear Mr. Scrooge, are you serious?'

'If you please,' said Scrooge. 'Not a farthing less. A great many back-payments are included in it, I assure you. Will you do me that favour?'

'My dear Sir,' said the other, shaking hands with him. 'I don't know what to say to such munifi-'

'Don't say anything, please,' retorted Scrooge. 'Come and see me. Will you come and see me?'

'I will!' cried the old gentleman. And it was clear he meant to do it.

'Thank'ee,' said Scrooge. 'I am much obliged to you. I thank you fifty times. Bless you!'

He went to church, and walked about the streets, and watched the people hurrying to and fro, and patted children on the head, and questioned beggars, and looked down into the kitchens of houses, and up to the windows; and found that everything could yield him pleasure. He had never dreamed that any walk – that anything – could give him so much happiness.

CHARLES DICKENS
A Christmas Carol

What sweeter music can we bring?

What sweeter music can we bring
Than a carol, for to sing
The birth of this our heavenly King?
Awake the voice! Awake the string:

We see him come, and know him ours,
Who with his sunshine and his showers
Turns all the patient ground to flowers.

Dark and dull night, fly hence away,
And give the honour to this day,
That sees December turned to May,
If we may ask the reason, say:

The darling of the world is come,
And fit it is we find a room
To welcome him. The nobler part
Of all the house here is the heart:

Which we will give him, and bequeath
This holly and this ivy wreath,
To do him honour who's our King,
And Lord of all this revelling:

ROBERT HERRICK

74

Christmas Morning in Italy

It was Christmas Day. However often I whispered it, I could scarcely credit so strange, so preposterous, so heavenly a fact. Christmas Day had indeed arrived. But how could it really, actually, in point of fact, have come, and I in bed as usual, in the same red flannel pyjamas as on any other night? Yet Christmas Day must come; one had long expected it, and here it was. Perhaps it was a dream.

But of a sudden the still dark was shaken and shattered and a-clamour with bells. Not the gay sweet chiming of an English church peal, but harsh, clanging, iron, tremendous, a very roar and tumult of noise. The great Roman brick tower of Sant Ambrogio in the large piazza outside the windows, the striped black and white tower of San Domenico in the small piazza up the street, the more distant, but patronal, Santa Caterian along the sea road beyond the town, the church of the Collegio up the hill path, the chapel of the convent school, all with one accord awoke to Christmas morning and clanged their summons to Mass. They were insistent, commanding, almost menacing. English bells, sweetly and uncertainly tumbling as they chime, seem to sing, *Come along to church, good people if you please, come along to church on Christmas Day*. These bells cry, *Venite, venite, il Signore v'aspetta, levatevi pronto, pronto, e fatte il dovere*.

But to me they only shouted, *Christmas Day! Christmas Day!*

Soon the piazza and streets were alive with hurrying feet, and with such resonant cries as Italians emit even between bed and Mass.

I crawled back under the bed-clothes and curled up to wait for Christmas Day. When it should be held to have fully arrived, we should all assemble on one bed and open the stockings. To me, lying in the clanging dark, forbidden to go and wake the others before it was light, the propitious and blest day seemed half the night away. How foolishly the others slept, oblivious of the jubilant occasion!

> *Full little thought they than*
> *That the mighty Pan*
> *Was kindly come to live with them below;*

> *Perhaps their loves, or else their sheep,*
> *Was all that did their silly thoughts so busie keep.*

Whatever it was, and regardless of the bells, they slept like pigs in straw.

ROSE MACAULAY
Personal Pleasures

Eternity framed in domesticity

In this vignette of Christmas dawn, which could describe almost any family, the Minivers and their children, Vin, Judy and Toby, are an echo of the Holy Family. Within the family we experience the same love, the same suffering – and the same joy.

To the banquet of real presents which was waiting downstairs, covered with a red and white dust-sheet, the stocking-toys, of course, were only an *apéritif*; but they had a special and exciting quality of their own. Perhaps it was the atmosphere in which they were opened – the chill, the black window-panes, the unfamiliar hour; perhaps it was the powerful charm of the miniature, of toy toys, of smallness squared; perhaps it was the sense of limitation within a strict form, which gives to both the filler and the emptier of a Christmas stocking something of the same enjoyment which is experienced by the writer and the reader of a sonnet; or perhaps it was merely that the spell of the old legend still persisted, even though for everybody in the room except Toby the legend itself was outworn.

There were cross-currents of pleasure, too: smiling glances exchanged by her and Vin [the eldest child] about the two younger children (she remembered suddenly, having been an eldest child, the unsurpassable sense of grandeur that such glances gave one); and by her and Clem, because they were both grown-ups; and by her and Judy, because they were both women; and by her and Toby, because they were both the kind that leaves the glass marble till the end. The room was laced with an invisible network of affectionate understanding.

This was one of the moments, thought Mrs Miniver, which paid off at a single stroke all the accumulations on the debit side of parenthood: the morning sickness and the quite astonishing pain; the pram in the passage, the cold, mulish glint in the cook's eye; the holiday nurse who had been in the best families; the pungent white mice, the shrivelled caterpillars; the plasticine on the door-handles, the face-flannels in the bathroom, the nameless horrors down the crevices of armchairs; the alarms and emergencies, the swallowed button, the inexplicable ear-ache, the ominous rash appearing on the eve of a journey; the school bills and the dentists' bills; the shortened step, the tempered pace, the emotional compromises, the divided loyalties, the adventures continually forsworn.

And now Vin was eating his tangerine, pig by pig; Judy had undressed the black baby and was putting on its frock again back to front; Toby was turning the glass marble round and round against the light, trying to count the squirls. There were sounds of movement in the house; they were within measurable distance of the blessed chink of early morning tea. Mrs Miniver looked towards the window. The dark sky had already paled a little in its frame of cherry-pink chintz. Eternity framed in domesticity. Never mind. One had to frame it in something, to see it at all.

JAN STRUTHER
Mrs Miniver

Christmas Expectations

Gradually there gathered the feeling of expectation. Christmas was coming. In the shed, at nights, a secret candle was burning, a sound of veiled voices was heard. The boys were learning the old mystery play of St George and Beelzebub. Twice a week, by lamplight, there was choir practice in the church, for the learning of old carols Brangwen wanted to hear. The girls went to these practices. Everywhere was a sense of mystery and rousedness. Everybody was preparing for something.

The time came near, the girls were decorating the church, with cold fingers binding holly and fir and yew about the pillars, till a new spirit was in the church, the stone broke out into dark, rich leaf, the arches put forth their buds, and cold flowers rose to blossom in the dim, mystic atmosphere. Ursula must weave mistletoe over the door, and over the screen, and hang a silver dove from a sprig of yew, till dusk came down, and the church was a grove.

In the cow-shed the boys were blacking their faces for a dress rehearsal; the turkey hung dead, with opened, speckled wings, in the dairy. The time was come to make pies, in readiness.

The expectation grew more tense. The star was risen into the sky, the songs, the carols were ready to hail it. The star was the sign in the sky. Earth too should give a sign. As evening drew on, hearts beat fast with anticipation, hands were full of ready gifts. There were the tremulously expectant words of the church service, the night was past and the morning was come, the gifts were given and received, joy and peace made a flapping of wings in each heart, there was a great burst of carols, the Peace of the World had dawned, strife had passed away, every hand was linked in hand, every heart was singing.

It was bitter, though, that Christmas day, as it drew on to evening and night, became a sort of bank holiday, flat and stale. The morning was so wonderful, but in the afternoon and the evening the ecstasy perished like a nipped thing, like a bud in false spring. Alas, that Christmas was only a domestic feast, a feast of sweetmeats and toys! Why did not the grown-ups also change their everyday hearts, and give way to ecstasy? Where was the ecstasy?

D H LAWRENCE
The Rainbow

3

Keeping Christmas

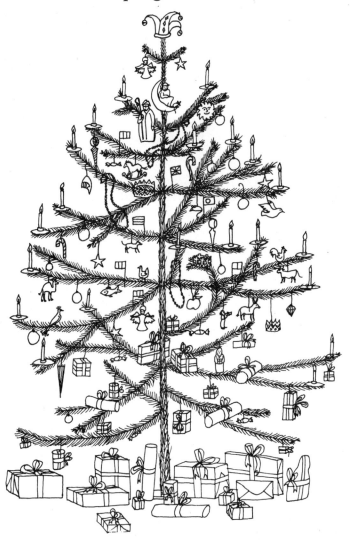

Keeping Christmas

It is now Christmas, and not a Cup of drinke must passe without
a Caroll, the Beasts, Fowle and Fish, come to generall execution,
and the Corne is ground to dust for the Bakehouse, and the
Pastry: Cards and Dice purge many a purse . . . now good cheere
and welcome, and God be with you, and I thanke you: and
against the new yeere, provide for the presents: the Lord of Mis-
rule is no meane man for his time, and the ghests of the high
Table must lacke no Wine: the lusty bloods must looke about
them like men, and piping the dauncing puts away much
melancholy: . . . a good fire heats all the house, and a full Almes-
basket makes the Beggars Prayers: . . . Swearers and Swaggerers
are sent away to the Alehouse, and unruly Wenches goe in
danger of Judgement: Musicians now make their Instruments
speake out, and a good song is worth the hearing. In summe, it
is holy time, a duty in Christians, for the remembrance of Christ,
and custome among friends, for the maintenance of good fellow-
ship: in briefe, I thus conclude of it: I hold it a memory of the
Heavens Love, and the worlds peace, the myrth of the honest,
and the meeting of the friendly.

NICHOLAS BRETON

Christmas Day at Sprigg's Farm

When Parson Ash stood up in the pulpit and opened the book
that contained a homily for every Sunday in the year, with
Christmas thrown in extra, no one, with the exception of Job
Stanberry, the clerk, went to sleep. The homily that was thrown
in extra was part of the Gentian Hill Christmas, and as such
worthy of attention. Most of the congregation knew it by heart
by this time; all but the last few words. 'And so, beloved brethren,' intoned Parson Ash, commencing at the peroration, 'let us
join our praises to those of the angels at his holy season, and
open our hearts in welcome to – ' And down came the Parson's
book on Job Stanberry's head as usual, so that still no one knew
what the last words were. Stella on the whole was glad because
she could employ herself all the way home thinking of all the
glory to which it was possible to open one's heart on Christmas
Day . . . The God of love. The Holy Child. Wonderful. Counsellor. The mighty Father. The Prince of Peace . . . It was enough
to make one's heart crack and break if one thought about it too
long.

The Christmas dinner at Weekaborough, which was shared
by several lonely neighbours and strolling vagabonds who had
come through the open door and not been refused, was colossal.
The kitchen was filled with steam and heat, laughter, noise and
bustle. It was the only part of Christmas that Stella did not
enjoy very much, and the fatigue of it left her with dark smudges
under her eyes. When the men were sitting round the great fire
with their pipes and glasses, and the women were stacking the
dishes and carrying them away to the scullery, Mother Sprigg
whispered, 'You can slip away, love, if you like. The parlour
fire is laid and you can light it. Here's the key.'

ELIZABETH GOUDGE
Gentian Hill

A Christmas Family Party

A Christmas family-party! We know nothing in nature more delightful! There seems a magic in the very name of Christmas. Petty jealousies and discords are forgotten: social feelings are awakened in bosoms to which they have long been strangers: father and son, or brother and sister, who have met and passed with averted gaze, or a look of cold recognition, for months before, proffer and return the cordial embrace, and bury their past animosities in their present happiness. Kindly hearts that have yearned towards each other, but have been withheld by false notions of pride and self-dignity, are again reunited, and all is kindness and benevolence! Would that Christmas lasted the whole year through, and that the prejudices and passions which deform our better nature, were never called into action among those to whom they should ever be strangers!

The Christmas family-party that we mean, is not a mere assemblage of relations, got up at a week or two's notice, originating this year, having no family precedent in the last, and not likely to be repeated in the next. It is an annual gathering of all the accessible members of the family, young or old, rich or poor; and all the children look forward to it, for two months beforehand, in a fever of anticipation . . .

CHARLES DICKENS
Sketches by Boz

Family Reunions

The discordance or discomfort complained of by modern critics, in the family reunion, is not due to that mystical focal fire having been left burning, but to its having been left to go cold. It is because cold fragments of a once living thing are clumsily lumped together; it is no argument against making the thing alive. Christmas toys are incongruously dangled before heavy and heathen uncles who wish they were playing golf. But that does not alter the fact that they might become much brighter and more intelligent if they knew how to play with toys; and they are horrible bores about golf. Their dullness is only the last deadly product of the mechanical progress of organized and professional sports, in that rigid world of routine outside the home. When they were children, behind closed doors in the home, it is probable that nearly every one of them had day-dreams and unwritten dramas that belonged to them as much as Hamlet belonged to Shakespeare or Pickwick to Dickens. How much more thrilling it would be if Uncle Henry, instead of describing in detail all the strokes with which he ought to have got out of the bunker, were to say frankly that he had been on a voyage to the end of the world and had just caught the Great Sea-Serpent. How much more truly intellectual would be the conversation of Uncle William if, instead of telling us the point to which he had reduced his handicap, he could still say with conviction that he was King of the Kangaroo Islands, or Chief of the Rango Dango Redskins . . .

G K CHESTERTON
The Thing

The Pooters' Christmas

December 19. The annual invitation came to spend Christmas with Carrie's mother – the usual family festive gathering, to which we always look forward. Lupin declined to go. I was astounded and expressed my surprise and disgust. Lupin then obliged us with the following Radical speech: 'I hate a family gathering at Christmas. What does it mean? Why someone says: "Ah! we miss poor Uncle James, who was here last year," and we all begin to snivel. Someone else says: "It's two years since poor Aunt Liz used to sit in that corner". Then we all begin to snivel again. Then another gloomy relation says: "Ah! I wonder whose turn it will be next?" Then we all snivel again, and proceed to eat and drink too much; and they don't discover until I get up that we have been seated thirteen at dinner.'

Lupin spends Christmas with the family of his fiancée.

Christmas Day. We caught the 10.20 train at Paddington, and spent a pleasant day at Carrie's mother's. The country was quite nice and pleasant, although the roads were sloppy. We dined in the middle of the day, just ten of us, and talked over old times. If everybody had a nice, *un*interfering mother-in-law, such as I have, what a deal of happiness there would be in the world. Being all in good spirits, I proposed her health; and I made, I think, a very good speech.

I concluded, rather neatly, by saying: 'On an occasion like this – whether relatives, friends or acquaintances – we are all inspired with good feelings towards each other. We are of one mind, and think only of love and friendship. Those who have quarrelled with absent friends should kiss and make it up. Those who happily have *not* fallen out, can kiss all the same.'

I saw the tears in the eyes of both Carrie and her mother, and must say I felt very flattered by the compliment. That dear old Reverend John Panzy Smith, who married us, made a most cheerful and amusing speech, and said he should act on my suggestion respecting the kissing. He then walked round the table and kissed all the ladies, including Carrie. Of course one did not object to this; but I was more than staggered when a young fellow named Moss, who was a stranger to me, and who had scarcely spoken a word through dinner, jumped up suddenly with a sprig of mistletoe, and exclaimed: 'Hulloh! I don't see why I shouldn't be in on this scene.' Before one could realize what he was about to do, he kissed Carrie and the rest of the ladies.

Fortunately the matter was treated as a joke, and we all laughed; but it was a dangerous experiment, and I felt very uneasy for a moment as to the result . . .

GEORGE AND WEEDON GROSSMITH
The Diary of a Nobody

A Quaker's Christmas, 1841

Christmas eve festivities. We were amongst a select few invited by Sterling's little people to witness the unfolding of a mighty mystery which has occupied their small brains for the last week. The folding doors of the drawing-room being thrown open, the inner room appeared like a blaze of light & luxury. In the centre stood a fir tree reaching nearly to the ceiling, covered in all direction with lighted tapers & various gay & glittering symbols, while pendant from the lower branches were numerous presents for children and guests. Papa's ingenious irony had placed a foolscap on the top, immediately overshadowing the man in the moon & the Pope of Rome; crowns & helmets, paper flags & necklaces sparkled amongst the foliage & we all, old children and young, gave ourselves up to the enthusism of the moment. My present was a beautiful ivory pen tipped with silver & wreathed with laurel, a most elegant compliment. A.M. & C. were given some very fine engravings. The excitement having somewhat subsided I put off a volcano in the garden. The abandon of the children to their supreme delight was beautiful.

BARCLAY FOX

A Victorian Christmas in Herefordshire

Tuesday, 24 December, Christmas Eve

Very hard frost. Brilliant sunshine on sparkling snow. After breakfast I went to the Old Weston to see the poor Davieses and comfort them concerning their child. On the road I met David Davies the father, the shepherd at the Weston, on his way to the village to order the coffin and to the Churchyard to mark out the ground for the grave. He told me it was not Andrew as I had been informed and supposed, but little Davie who was dead. The father seemed greatly distressed and indignant because he thought the child's life had been thrown away by some mistake of the doctor. I went on to the house of mourning. Margaret Davies seemed very glad to see me and her humble gratitude for my visit was most touching. She took me upstairs into the room where the dead child was lying on the bed and turned down the sheet from his face. I never saw death look so beautiful. There was no bandage round the chin. The pretty innocent child face looked as peaceful and natural as if the child were asleep and the dark curls lay upon the little pillow. I could hardly believe he was dead. Leaving the face still uncovered the poor mother knelt with me by the little bedside while I prayed for them all. She was deeply touched and most humbly grateful. Before I left the room I stooped and kissed the child's forehead, and the mother did the same. It was as cold and as hard as marble. This is always a fresh surprise. I had not touched death for more than 30 years, and it brought back the sudden shock that I felt when as a child I was taken into a room at Hardenhuish Rectory where our little sister lay dead and was told to touch her hand.

Margaret Davies told me that before little Davie died he saw a number of people and some pretty children dancing in a beautiful garden and heard some sweet music. Then someone seems to have called him for he answered, 'What do you want with me?' He also saw beautiful birds, and the men of Weston (who carried him to his funeral). He thought his little sister Margaret was throwing ice and snow on him. (The snow fell on the coffin at the burial.) On the road I overtook Miss Stokes and went into the Old Court with her but before Kate could come and speak to me my nose began to bleed and I was obliged to fly.

Wednesday, Christmas Day

Very hard frost last night. At Presteign the thermometer fell to 2 degrees, showing 30 degrees of frost. At Monnington it fell to 4. Last night is said to have been the coldest night for 100 years. The windows of the house and Church were so thick with frost rime that we could not see out. We could not look through the Church windows all day. Snow lay on the ground and the day was dark and gloomy with a murky sky. A fair morning congregation considering the weather. By Miss Newton's special desire Dora and I went to the Cottage to eat our Christmas dinner at 1.30 immediately after service.

Immediately after dinner I had to go back to the church for the funeral of little Davie of the Old Weston who died on Monday was fixed for 2.15. The weather was dreadful, the snow driving in blinding clouds and the walking tiresome. Yet the funeral was only 20 minutes late. The Welcome Home, as it chimed softly and slowly to greet the little pilgrim coming to his rest, sounded bleared and muffled through the thick snowy air. The snow fell thickly all through the funeral service and at the service by the grave a kind woman offered her umbrella which a kind young fellow came and held over my head. The woman and man were Mrs Richards and William Jackson. I asked the poor mourners to come in and rest and warm themselves but they would not and went into Church. The poor father, David Davies the shepherd, was crying bitterly for the loss of his little lamb. Owing to the funeral it was rather late before we began the afternoon service. There were very few people in Church beside the mourners. The afternoon was very dark. I was obliged to move close to the great south window to read the Lessons and could hardly see even then. I preached from Luke ii.7. 'There was no room for them in the inn,' and connected the little bed in the churchyard in which we had laid Davie to rest with the manger cradle at Bethlehem.

In spite of the heavy and deep snow there was a fair congregation at Brobury Church. I walked there with Powell. The water was out in Brobury lane. As we came back a thaw had set in and rain fell. By Miss Newton's special wish I went to the Cottage and spent the evening with Dora. The Cottage servants had invited the Vicarage servants to tea and supper and they came into the drawing room after supper and sang some Christmas Carols.

FRANCIS KILVERT

Christmastide

The rain-shafts splintered on me
  As despondently I strode;
The twilight gloomed upon me
  And bleared the blank high-road
Each bush gave forth, when blown on
  By gusts in shower and shower,
A sigh, as it were sown on
  In handfuls by a sower.

A cheerful voice called, nigh me,
  'A merry Christmas, friend!' –
There rose a figure by me,
  Walking with townward trend,
A sodden tramp's, who, breaking
  Into thin song, bore straight
Ahead, direction taking
  Toward the Casual's gate.

THOMAS HARDY

Christmas Bells

I heard the bells on Christmas Day
Their old familiar carols play,
   And wild and sweet
   The words repeat
Of Peace on earth, Good-will to men!

And thought how, as the day had come,
The belfries of all Christendom
   Had rolled along
   The unbroken song
Of Peace on earth, Good-will to men!

Till ringing, singing on its way,
The world revolved from night to day,
   A voice, a chime,
   A chant sublime,
Of Peace on earth, Good-will to men!

Then from each black accursed mouth,
The cannon thundered in the South,
   And with the sound
   The carols drowned,
The Peace on earth, Good-will to men!

And in despair I bowed my head;
'There is no peace on earth,' I said,
   'For hate is strong
   And mocks the song
Of Peace on earth, Good-will to men!'

Then pealed the bells more loud and deep:
'God is not dead, nor doth he sleep!
   The Wrong shall fail,
   The Right prevail,
With Peace on earth, Good-will to men!'

HENRY WADSWORTH LONGFELLOW

An Edwardian Vicarage Christmas

It was not like the Christmases at St Leonard's-on-Sea when, for days beforehand, the bell never stopped ringing as gifts of all kinds were delivered – but especially useful, helpful presents from the parishioners. In those days the tradespeople with whom you dealt sent presents: a turkey from the butcher; a box of crystallized fruits or chocolates from the grocer; fruit from the greengrocer. Even the local undertaker sent a present of wine. Tradespeople's presents still turned up, but at Eastbourne there were fewer presents from the parishioners, though the children's father received enough and from such unexpected sources to make him feel quite overcome.

'How kind they are, dear people,' he said as he received for his wife yet another pot plant or, for the children, chocolates or something for himself. 'I really expected nothing, my first Christmas here.'

Then off the children's father would dash, his arms full of little books on Christian subjects which he had signed for his friends, for it was a strict rule in the family that for a present received one was sent. Even when they were tiny the children were taught this and would work laboriously at home-made gifts. Granny, who even when the children were small was not much good at getting about, still cherished a book-marker made by Victoria just before her sixth birthday. Its text, in cross stitch, said *Hop on hop ever*. Even now, though they had less time, the girls made many Christmas presents, some of which were put away as emergency gifts to send to the unexpected giver: simple presents such as lavender bags; emery cushions for rusty needles; pen-wipers and needle-books; but, no doubt being home-made, they pleased.

There were some things that were new about the Eastbourne Christmas. Always the family had been used to carol singers who came into the hall to sing and afterwards were given ginger wine and mince pies. But this year, as well as carol singers, hand-bell ringers arrived. They stood in a circle pealing out the old favourites while the family sat on the stairs to listen.

'There is something about bells,' Isobel said after the bell-ringers had gone. 'As they rang I sort of felt Christmas come into the house.' . . .

Another feature of that Christmas was the curate. Curates came and curates went and, except on special occasions, the children seldom saw them to talk to because their father kept his curates' noses to the grindstone. But the curates usually came to Christmas lunch and, unless they had anywhere better to go, stayed on for tea and the Christmas tree – and dull and shy the children found them.

That year the curate – a man called Plimsol, known to the children as Mr Cassock because he seldom seemed to wear anything else – came to lunch. Right away he set a new standard for curates by arriving with five boxes of Fuller's chocolates. A box of chocolates of their own was highly thought of by the children, for most of the boxes received were family boxes and were stored in a cupboard to be passed round before bed, when each child was allowed one. So individual boxes from which the children were allowed, with permission, to help themselves were much valued. But that was not all; when the crackers were pulled Mr Plimsol found a blue sun-bonnet in his and not only put it on but sang: 'Oh, what have you got for dinner, Mrs Bond?' in a delightfully silly way.

'Bags I you for my team for charades this evening,' said John.

Always for Christmas tea and the tree afterwards the vicarage doors were thrown open to those who were lonely or had nowhere else to go. Annie [the maid], on hearing the Christmas arrangements, made a remark which became a family quotation: 'As at Sandringham'.

Either because of the success of Mr Plimsol in the charades or because of some special quality surrounded that Christmas, it stayed in the children's memory.

Their mother always decorated the tree and they were never allowed to see it until the candles were lit. That year the tree stood in the small annexe to the drawing-room – a perfect place, because there were curtains which could be drawn back when the tree was to be seen in all its glory. That year there were about fifteen waifs and strays, mostly women, all rather shy and sad while they drank tea and ate Victoria's birthday – now the Christmas – cake.

When the tea was cleared, Annie and Hester joined the party, and soon everyone was circling the tree singing *The First Nowell* and then *Good King Wenceslaus*, with John singing the King's verses and Victoria the page's. Then came the time to strip the tree. The majority of the parcels were for the family of course, but no one was allowed to feel left out, so there were plenty of little gifts for the guests. Annie and Hester (Miss Herbert went to a brother for Christmas) had presents from every member of the family and, as well as proper presents from the children's parents, each received an afternoon apron. Annie said when she opened her parcel:

'Thank you, madam. It will save you buying me one for when you want me to bring in tea on Hester's day out.'

The present-giving over and the wrappings swept up, the charades started and, as had been hoped, Mr Plimsol proved a natural comic. It was lovely to see the lonely, rather sad people who had arrived, mopping the tears of laughter off their cheeks.

Then there was more carol singing and then the guests were in the hall putting on their wraps, and another Christmas Day was over.

NOEL STREATFEILD
A Vicarage Family

Christmas Day. The Family Sitting

In the days of Caesar Augustus
   There went forth this decree:
Si quis rectus et justus
   Liveth in Galilee,
Let him go up to Jerusalem
   And pay his scot to me.

There are passed one after the other
   Christmases fifty-three,
Since I sat here with my mother
   And heard the great decree:
How they went up to Jerusalem
   Out of Galilee.

They have passed one after the other;
   Father and mother died,
Brother and sister and brother
   Taken and sanctified.
I am left alone in the sitting,
   With none to sit beside.

On the fly-leaves of these old prayer-books
   The childish writings fade,
Which show that once they were their books
   In the days when prayer was made
For other kings and princesses,
   William and Adelaide.

The pillars are twisted with holly,
   And the font is wreathed with yew.
Christ forgive me for folly,
   Youth's lapses – not a few,
For the hardness of my middle life,
   For age's fretful view.

Cotton-wool letters on scarlet,
   All the ancient lore,
Tell how the chieftains starlit

To Bethlehem came to adore;
To hail Him King in the manger,
  Wonderful, Counsellor.

The bells ring out in the steeple
  The gladness of erstwhile,
And the children of other people
  Are walking up the aisle;
They brush my elbow in passing,
  Some turn to give me a smile.

Is the almond blossom bitter?
  Is the grasshopper heavy to bear?
Christ make me happier, fitter
  To go to my own over there;
Jerusalem the Golden,
  What bliss beyond compare!

My Lord, where I have offended
  Do Thou forgive it me.
That so when, all being ended,
  I hear Thy last decree,
I may go up to Jerusalem
  Out of Galilee.

JOHN MEADE FALKNER

Christmas in Biafra (1969)

This sunken-eyed moment wobbling
down the rocky steepness on broken
bones slowly fearfully to hideous
concourse of gathering sorrows in the valley
will yet become in another year a lost
Christmas irretrievable in the heights
its exploding inferno transmuted
by cosmic distances to the peacefulness
of a cool twinkling star . . . To death-cells
of that moment came faraway sounds of other
men's carols floating on crackling waves
mocking us. With regret? Hope? Longing? None of
these, strangely, not even despair rather
distilling pure transcendental hate . . .

Beyond the hospital gate
the good nuns had set up a manger
of palms to house a fine plastercast
scene at Bethlehem. The Holy
Family was central, serene, the Child
Jesus plump wise-looking and rose-cheeked; one
of the magi in keeping with legend
a black Othello in sumptuous robes. Other
figures of men and angels stood
at well-appointed distances from
the heart of the divine miracle
and the usual cattle gazed on
in holy wonder . . .

Poorer than the poor worshippers
before her who had paid their homage
with pitiful offering of new aluminium
coins that few traders would take and
a frayed five-shilling note she only
crossed herself and prayed open-eyed. Her
infant son flat like a dead lizard
on her shoulder his arms and legs
cauterized by famine was a miracle

of its kind. Large sunken eyes
stricken past boredom to a flat
unrecognizing glueyness moped faraway
motionless across her shoulder . . .

Now her adoration over
she turned him around and pointed
at those pretty figures of God
and angels and men and beasts –
a spectacle to stir the heart
of a child. But all he vouchsafed
was one slow deadpan look of total
unrecognition and he began again
to swivel his enormous head away
to mope as before at his empty distance . . .
She shrugged her shoulders, crossed
herself again and took him away.

CHINUA ACHEBE

Christmas in Prison

From the Christian point of view there is no special problem about Christmas in a prison cell. For many people in this building it will probably be a more sincere and genuine occasion than in places where nothing but the name is kept. That misery, suffering, poverty, loneliness, helplessness and guilt mean something quite different in the eyes of God from what they mean in the judgement of man, that God will approach where men turn away, that Christ was born in a stable because there was no room for him in the inn – these are things that a prisoner can understand better than other people; for him they really are glad tidings . . .

DIETRICH BONHOEFFER
Letters and Papers from Prison

Christmas Nostalgia

There are people who will tell you that Christmas is not to them what it used to be: that each succeeding Christmas has found some cherished hope, or happy prospect, of the year before, dimmed or passed away, and that the present only serves to remind them of reduced circumstances and straitened incomes – of the feasts they once bestowed on hollow friends, and of the cold looks that meet them now, in adversity and misfortune. Never heed such dismal reminiscences. There are few men who have lived long enough in the world, who cannot call up such thoughts any day in the year. Then do not select the merriest of the three hundred and sixty-five, for your doleful recollections, but draw your chair nearer the blazing fire – fill the glass and send round the song – and if your room be smaller than it was a dozen years ago, or if your glass be filled with reeking punch, instead of sparkling wine, put a good face on the matter, and empty it off-hand, and fill another, and troll off the old ditty you used to sing, and thank God it's no worse . . . Reflect upon your present blessings – of which every man has many – not on your past misfortunes, of which all men have some. Fill your glass again, with a merry face and contented heart. Out upon it, but your Christmas shall be merry, and your New Year a happy one.

CHARLES DICKENS
Sketches by Boz

No Christmas

The Puritans came to power in 1640 but Christmas was not immediately abolished. The Presbyterians' dislike of the observance of Christmas finally erupted in 1644, when Christmas Day fell upon the newly appointed fast day, and an order was given on 19 December to suppress it.

Whereas some doubts have been raised, whether the next fast shall be celebrated, because it falls on the day which heretofore was usually called the feast of the nativity of our Saviour; the lords and commons in parliament assembled to order and ordain, that public notice be given, that the fast appointed to be kept the last Wednesday in every month ought to be observed, till it be otherwise ordered by both houses; and that this day in particular is to be kept with the more solemn humiliation, because it may call to remembrance our sins, and the sins of our forefathers, who have turned this feast, pretending to the memory of Christ, into an extreme forgetfulness of him, by giving liberty to carnal and sensual delights, being contrary to the life which Christ led here on earth, and to the spiritual life of Christ in our souls, for the sanctifying and saving whereof, Christ was pleased both to take a human life, and to lay it down again.

On Christmas Day itself, Edmund Calamy preached before the House of Lords:

This day is commonly called Christmas-day, a day that has heretofore been much abused in superstition and profaneness. It is not easy to say, whether the superstition has been greater, or the profaneness . . . and truly, I think the superstition and profaneness of the day are so rooted in it, that there is no way to reform it, but by dealing with it as Hezekiah did with the brazen serpent. This year God, by his providence, has buried it in a fast, and I hope it will never rise again.

In Dessexshire as it Befel

In Dessexshire as it befel
A farmer there as I knew well
On a Christmas day as it happened so
Down in the meadows he went to plough.

As he was a ploughing on so fast
Our Saviour Christ came by at last;
He said, O man, why dost thou plough
So hard as it do blow and snow?

The man he answered the Lord with speed,
For to work we have great need,
If we wasn't to work all on that day
We should want some other way.

For his hands did tremble and pass to and fro,
He ran so fast that he could not plough;
And the ground did open and let him in
Before he could repent his sin.

His wife and children were out at play;
And all the world consumed at last.
And his beasts and cattle all died away
For breaking of the Lord's birthday.

ANONYMOUS

A Puritan Christmas

Dec. 25, 1696. We bury our little daughter. In the chamber, Joseph in course reads Ecclesiastes 3rd a time to be born and a time to die – Elisabeth, Rev. 22. Hanah, the 38th Psalm. I speak to each, as God helped, to our mutual comfort I hope. I ordered Sam to read the 102 Psalm. Elisha Cooke, Edw. Hutchinson, John Baily, and Josia Willard bear my little daughter to the Tomb.

Note. Twas wholly dry, and I went at noon to see in what order things were set; and there I was entertained with a view of, and converse with, the Coffins of my dear Father Hull, Mother Hull, Cousin Quinsey, and my Six Children: for the little posthumous was now took up and set in upon that that stands on John's: so are three, one upon another twice, on the bench at the end. My Mother lies on a lower bench, at the end, with head to her Husband's head: and I ordered little Sarah to be set on her Grandmother's feet. 'Twas an awfull yet pleasing Treat; Having said, The Lord knows who shall be brought hither next, I came away.

* * *

April 1, 1719. In the morning I dehorted Sam Hirst and Grindal Rawson from playing Idle Tricks because 'twas first of April; They were the greatest fools that did so. New England Men came hither to avoid anniversary days, the keeping of them, such as the 25th of Dec. How displeasing must it be to God, the giver of our Time, to keep anniversary days to play the fool with ourselves and others . . .

SAMUEL SEWALL

Out upon Merry Christmas!

'A Merry Christmas, uncle! God save you!' cried a cheerful voice. It was the voice of Scrooge's nephew, who came upon him so quickly that this was the first intimation he had of his approach.

'Bah!' said Scrooge. 'Humbug!'

He had so heated himself with rapid walking in the fog and frost, this nephew of Scrooge's, that he was all in a glow; his face was ruddy and handsome; his eyes sparkled, and his breath smoked again.

'Christmas a humbug, uncle!' said Scrooge's nephew. 'You don't mean that, I am sure.'

'I do,' said Scrooge. 'Merry Christmas! What right have you to be merry? What reason have you to be merry? You're poor enough.'

'Come, then,' returned the nephew, gayly. 'What right have you to be dismal? What reason have you to be morose? You're rich enough.'

Scrooge having no better answer ready on the spur of the moment, said, 'Bah!' again; and followed it up with 'Humbug.'

'Don't be cross, uncle,' said the nephew.

'What else can I be,' returned the uncle, 'when I live in such a world of fools as this? Merry Christmas! Out upon Merry Christmas! What's Christmas time to you but a time for paying bills without money; a time for finding yourself a year older, but not an hour richer; a time for balancing your books and having every item in 'em through a round dozen of months presented dead against you? If I could work my will,' said Scrooge, indignantly, 'every idiot who goes about with "Merry Christmas", on his lips, should be boiled with his own pudding, and buried with a stake of holly through his heart. He should!'

'Uncle!' pleaded the nephew.

'Nephew!' returned the uncle, sternly, 'keep Christmas in your own way, and let me keep it in mine.'

'Keep it!' repeated Scrooge's nephew. 'But you don't keep it.'

'Let me leave it alone, then,' said Scrooge. 'Much good may it do you! Much good it has ever done you!'

'There are many things from which I have derived good, but which I have not profited, I dare say,' returned the nephew:

'Christmas among the rest. But I am sure I have always thought of Christmas time, when it has come round – apart from the veneration due to its sacred name and origin, if anything belonging to it can be apart from that – as a good time: a kind, forgiving, charitable, pleasant time: the only time I know of, in the long calendar of the year, when men and women seem by one consent to open up their shut-up hearts freely, and to think of people below them as if they really were fellow-passengers to the grave, and not another race of creatures bound on other journeys. And therefore, uncle, though it has never put a scrap of gold or silver in my pocket, I believe that it *has* done me good, and *will* do me good; and I say, God bless it!'

The clerk in the Tank involuntarily applauded: becoming immediately sensible of the impropriety, he poked the fire, and extinguished the last frail spark forever.

'Let me hear another sound from *you*,' said Scrooge, 'and you'll keep your Christmas by losing your situation.'

CHARLES DICKENS
A Christmas Carol

The Tranter's Christmas Party

The guests had all assembled, and the tranter's party had reached that degree of development which accords with ten o'clock p.m. in rural assemblies. At that hour the sound of a fiddle in process of tuning was heard from the inner pantry.

'That's Dick,' said the tranter. 'That lad's crazy for a jig.'

'Dick! Now I cannot – really, I cannot have any dancing at all till Christmas-day is out,' said old William emphatically. 'When the clock ha' done striking twelve, dance as much as ye like.'

'Well, I must say there's reason in that, William,' said Mrs Penny. 'If you do have a party on Christmas-night, 'tis only fair and honourable to the sky-folk to have it a sit-still party. Jigging parties be all very well on the Devil's holidays; but a jigging party looks suspicious now. O yes; stop till the clock strikes, young folk – so say I.'

It happened that some warm mead accidentally got into Mr Spink's head about this time.

'Dancing,' he said, 'is a most strengthening, livening, and courting movement, 'specially with a little beverage added! And dancing is good. But why disturb what is ordained, Richard and Reuben, and the company zhinerally? Why, I ask, as far as that do go?'

'Then nothing till after twelve,' said William.

Though Reuben and his wife ruled on social points, religious questions were mostly disposed of by the old man, whose firmness on this head quite counterbalanced a certain weakness in his handling of domestic matters. The hopes of the younger members of the household were therefore relegated to a distance of one hour and three-quarters – a result that took visible shape in them by a remote and listless look about the eyes – the singing of songs being permitted in the interim.

At five minutes to twelve the soft tuning was again heard in the back quarters; and when at length the clock had whizzed forth the last stroke, Dick appeared ready primed, and the instruments were boldly handled; old William very readily taking the bass-viol from its accustomed nail, and touching the strings as irreligiously as could be desired.

✳   ✳   ✳

'I like a party very well once in a while,' said Mrs Dewy, leaving off the adorned tones she had been bound to use throughout the evening and returning to the natural marriage voice; 'but, Lord, 'tis such a sight of heavy work next day! What with the dirty plates, and knives and forks, and dust and smother, and bits kicked off your furniture, and I don't know what all, why a body could a'most wish there were no such things as Christmases . . . '

THOMAS HARDY
Under the Greenwood Tree

Christmas must go

Christmas is utterly unsuited to the modern world. It presupposes the possibility of families being united, or reunited, and even of the men and women who chose each other being on speaking terms. Thus thousands of young adventurous spirits, ready to face the facts of human life, and encounter the vast variety of men and women as they really are, ready to fly to the ends of the earth and tolerate every alien or accidental quality in cannibals or devil-worshippers, are cruelly forced to face an hour, nay sometimes even two hours, in the society of Uncle George; or some aunt from Cheltenham whom they do not particularly like. Such abominable tortures cannot be tolerated in a time like ours. That larger brotherhood, that truer sensibility, has already taught every spirited young lady (of sufficient wealth and leisure) to be thrilled at the prospect of having breakfast with a gun-man, lunch with a Sheik, and dinner with an Apache in Paris. It is intolerable that such sensibility should suffer the shock of the unexpected appearance of her own mother, or possibly her own child. It was never supposed that Parents were included in the great democratic abstraction called People. It was never supposed that brotherhood could extend to brothers.

Anyhow, Christmas is unsuited to modern life; its concentration in the household was conceived without allowing for the size and convenience of the modern hotel; its inheritance of ceremonial ignored the present convention of unconventionality; its appeal to childhood was in conflict with the more liberal conception; that Bright Young Things should always feel as if they were old and talk as if they were dull . . .

. . . Anyhow, it is unnecessary to extend the list of evidences that Christmas does not fit in with this fuller and more liberated life. Christmas must go. Christmas is utterly unsuited to the great future that is now opening before us. Christmas is not founded on the great communal conception which can only find its final expression in Communism. Christmas does not really help the higher and healthier and more vigorous expansion of Capitalism. Christmas cannot be expected to fit in with modern hopes of a great social future. Christmas is a contradiction of modern thought. Christmas is an obstacle to modern progress.

Rooted in the past, and even the remote past, it cannot assist a world in which the ignorance of history is the only clear evidence of the knowledge of science. Born among miracles reported from two thousand years ago, it cannot expect to impress that sturdy common sense which can withstand the plainest and most palpable evidence for miracles happening at this moment. Dealing with matters purely psychic, it naturally has no interest for psychologists; having been the moral atmosphere of millions for more than sixteen centuries, it is of no interest to an age concerned with averages and statistics. It is concerned with the happiest of births and is the chief enemy of Eugenics; it carries along with it a tradition of voluntary virginity, yet it contains no really practical hints for compulsory sterilisation. At every point it is found to be in opposition to that great onward movement, by which we know that ethics will evolve into something that is more ethical and free from all ethical distinctions. Christmas is not modern; Christmas is not Marxian; Christmas is not made on the pattern of that great age of the Machine, which promises to the masses an epoch of even greater happiness and prosperity than that to which it has brought the masses at this moment. Christmas is medieval; having arisen in the earlier days of the Roman Empire. Christmas is a superstition. Christmas is a survival of the past.

But why go on piling up the praises of Christmas? All its gifts and glories are externally symbolised in that fact already sufficiently summarised; that it is a nuisance to all the people talking the particular nonsense of our own time. It is an irritation to all men who have lost their instincts; which is very truly the intellectual equivalent of losing their senses. It is a perpetual annoyance to the cads who are not only captains of industry, but captains of information and international news, and everything else in the present paradise of cads. It is a challenge to caddishness, because it reminds us of a more gracious world of courtesy; and of customs which assumed a sort of dignity in human relations. It is a puzzle to pedants whose cold hatred involves them in a continual contradiction; who are distracted between denouncing Christians because it is a Mass, or purely Popish mummery, and trying to prove at the same time that it is entirely heathen, and was once as admirable as everything else invented by the pirates of heathen Scandinavia. It stands up unbroken and baffling; for us one thing, for them a confusion

112

of inconsistencies; and it judges the modern world. Christmas must go. It is going. In fact it is going strong.

G K CHESTERTON
G K's Weekly, 7 Dec 1933

4

To Candlemas and Beyond

Why art thou troubled, Herod?

Why art thou troubled, Herod? what vain fear
   Thy blood-revolving breast to rage doth move?
Heaven's King, who doffs himself weak flesh to wear,
   Comes not to rule in wrath, but serve in love;
Nor would he this thy feared crown from thee tear,
   But give thee a better with himself above.
      Poor jealousy! why should he wish to prey
      Upon thy crown, who gives his own away?

Make to thy reason, man, and mock thy doubts;
   Look how below thy fears their causes are;
Thou art a soldier, Herod; send thy scouts,
   See how he's furnished for so feared a war.
What armour does he wear? a few thin clouts.
   His trumpets? tender cries. His men, to dare
      So much? rude shepherds. What his steeds? alas,
      Poor beasts! a slow ox and a simple ass.

RICHARD CRASHAW

The New-Yeeres Gift

Let others look for pearle and gold,
Tissues, or tabbies manifold:
One onely lock of that sweet hay
Whereon the blessed babie lay,
Or one poore swadling-clout, shall be
The richest new-yeeres gift to me.

ROBERT HERRICK

New Year's Eve

Of all sound of all bells – (bells, the music nighest bordering upon heaven) – most solemn and touching is the peal which rings out the Old Year. I never hear it without a gathering-up of my mind to a concentration of all the images that have been diffused over the past twelvemonth; all I have done or suffered, performed or neglected, in that regretted time. I begin to know its worth, as when a person dies. It takes a personal colour; nor was it a poetical flight in a contemporary, when he exclaimed –

I saw the skirts of the departing Year.

It is no more than what in sober sadness every one of us seems to be conscious of, in that awful leave-taking. I am sure I felt it, and all felt it with me, last night; though some of my companions affected rather to manifest an exhilaration at the birth of the coming year, than any very tender regrets for the decease of its predecessor. But I am none of those who –

Welcome the coming, speed the parting guest.

I am naturally, beforehand, shy of novelties; new books, new faces, new years, – from some mental twist which makes it difficult in me to face the prospective. I have almost ceased to hope; and am sanguine only in the prospects of other (former) years. I plunge into foregone visions and conclusions. I encounter pell-mell with past disappointments. I am armour-proof against old discouragements. I forgive, or overcome in fancy, old adversaries. I play over again *for love*, as the gamesters phrase it, games for which I once paid so dear . . .

The elders, with whom I was brought up, were of a character not likely to let slip the sacred observance of any old institution; and the ringing out of the Old Year was kept by them with circumstances of peculiar ceremony. – In those days the sound of those midnight chimes, though it seemed to raise hilarity in all around me, never failed to bring a train of pensive imagery into my fancy . . .

CHARLES LAMB

A New-year's gift sent to Sir Simeon Steward

No news of Navies burnt at seas;
No noise of late spawned *Tittyries*,
No closet plot, or open vent,
That frights men with a Parliament:
No new device, or late found trick,
To read by the Stars, the Kingdom's sick:
No gin to catch the State, or wring
The free-born Nostrils of the King,
We send you; but here a jolly
Verse crowned with Ivy and with Holly:
That tells of Winter's Tales and Mirth,
That Milk-maids make about the heart,
Of Christmas sports, the Wassail-bowl,
That's tossed up, after *Fox-i' th'hole*:
Of *Blind-man-buff*, and of the care
That young men have to shoe the *Mare*:
Of Twelfth-tide Cakes, of Peas and Beans,
Wherewith ye make those merry Scenes,
When as ye choose your King and Queen,
And cry out, *Hey for our town green*.
Of Ash-heaps, in the which ye use
Husbands and Wives by streaks to choose:
Of crackling Laurel, which fore-sounds
A Plenteous harvest to your grounds:
Of these, and such like things, for shift,
We send in stead of New-'s gift.
Read then, and when your faces shine
With bucksome meat and capering Wine:
Remember us in Cups full crowned,
And let our City-health go round,
Quite through the young maids and the men,
To the ninth number, if not ten;
Until the fired Chestnuts leap
For joy, to see the fruits ye reap,
From the plump Chalice, and the Cup,
That tempts till it be tossed up:
Then as ye sit about your embers,
Call not to mind those fled Decembers;

But think on these, that are to appear,
As Daughters to the instant year:
Sit crowned with Rose-buds, and carouse,
Till *Liber Pater* twirls the house
About your ears; and lay upon
The year (your cares) that's fled and gone.
And let the russet Swains the Plough
And Harrow hang up resting now;
And to the Bagpipe all address;
Till sleep takes place of weariness.
And thus, throughout, with Christmas plays
Frolic the full twelve Holy-days.

ROBERT HERRICK

Ring out, wild bells

Ring out, wild bells, to the wild sky,
  The flying cloud, the frosty light:
  The year is dying in the night;
Ring out, wild bells, and let him die.

Ring out the old, ring in the new,
  Ring, happy bells, across the snow:
  The year is going, let him go;
Ring out the false, ring in the true.

Ring out the grief that saps the mind,
  For those that here we see no more;
  Ring out the feud of rich and poor,
Ring in redress to all mankind.

Ring out a slowly dying cause,
  And ancient forms of party strife;
  Ring in the nobler modes of life,
With sweeter manners, purer laws.

Ring out the want, the care, the sin,
  The faithless coldness of the times;
  Ring out, ring out thy mournful rhymes,
But ring the fuller minstrel in.

Ring out false pride in place and blood,
  The civic slander and the spite;
  Ring in the love of truth and right,
Ring in the common love of good.

Ring out old shapes of foul disease;
  Ring out the narrowing lust of gold;
  Ring out the thousand wars of old,
Ring in the thousand years of peace.

Ring in the valiant man and free,
    The larger heart, the kindlier hand;
    Ring out the darkness of the land,
Ring in the Christ that is to be.

ALFRED, LORD TENNYSON

New Year's Eve

'I have finished another year,' said God,
   'In grey, green, white, and brown;
I have strewn the leaf upon the sod,
Sealed up the worm within the clod,
   And let the last sun down.'

'And what's the good of it?' I said,
   'What reasons made you call
From formless void this earth we tread,
When nine-and-ninety can be read
   Why nought should be at all?

'Yea, Sire; why shaped you us, "who in
   This tabernacle groan" –
If ever a joy be found herein,
Such joy no man had wished to win
   If he had never known!'

Then he: 'My labours – logicless –
   You may explain; not I:
Sense-sealed I have wrought, without a guess
That I evolved a Consciousness
   To ask for reasons why.

'Strange that ephemeral creatures who
   By my own ordering are,
Should see the shortness of my view,
Use ethic tests I never knew,
   Or made provision for!'

He sank to raptness as of yore,
   And opening New Year's Day
Wove it by rote as theretofore,
And went on working evermore
   In his unweeting way.

THOMAS HARDY

What the bird said early in the year

I heard in Addison's Walk a bird sing clear
'This year the summer will come true. This year. This year.

'Winds will not strip the blossom from the apple trees
This year, nor want of rain destroy the peas.

'This year time's nature will no more defeat you,
Nor all the promised moments in their passing cheat you.

'This time they will not lead you round and back
To Autumn, one year older, by the well-worn track.

'This year, this year, as all these flowers foretell,
We shall escape the circle and undo the spell.

'Often deceived, yet open once again your heart,
Quick, quick, quick, quick! – the gates are drawn apart.'

C S LEWIS

Resolutions

Victoria was sitting on Isobel's bed. It was New Year's Eve and the girls were waiting to hear the bells ring in 1911. Isobel put the alarm clock she had been given as a Christmas present back on the bedside pedestal – something found in every bedroom in those days.

'Lucky I had this or we'd never have been awake. Next year I shan't be here, for I suppose I'll go with Mummy to the midnight service, as I'll be confirmed by then.'

'Passing from the old year to the new upon your knees,' Victoria agreed, quoting what yearly her father said in church. 'Isn't it awful how old you are getting? I hate to think of you being confirmed, it means you won't be there for stockings on Christmas Day. You'll come in from church as if you were a grown-up.'

'Well, I will be fifteen in August. That's almost old enough to be married. Mummy married Daddy when she was seventeen.'

Victoria looked at Isobel.

'You don't look any different. Your chest sticks out more, that's all. Mine doesn't.'

'Well, you're only just thirteen – I expect it will begin this year. What resolutions are you making?'

Victoria sighed.

'The same as usual, but I don't know why I make them, for I break them right away. Tonight I will vow not to argue, always to get up the moment I'm called, not to fight with Louise, and to work so hard at school I'll get a good report. But I'm very despairing about keeping any of them.'

Isobel looked again at her clock.

'We haven't long.' She took a piece of paper from under her pillow. 'I've written mine down. Not to mind when Miss Herbert fusses; not to mind when I'm ill; not to mind not going to a proper art school.' She hesitated then folded the paper. 'That's all.'

Victoria made a pounce.

'It's *not* all. Let me see.'

But Isobel had the paper tight in her folded hand.

'You can't see – anyway it's time. Go and open your window

so you can hear the bells, and don't quite shut my door so I can hear them too.'

Victoria flung open her window. The bells of all the churches in Eastbourne were ringing, and from down the street there were voices shouting greetings. Into the night Victoria called her resolutions in the form of a prayer.

'Please, God, don't let me argue once with anyone, not even Miss Herbert. And help me to get up the very minute I'm called. And don't let me fight with Louise, however awful she is. And make me work harder at school however mean Miss French was about my ankle, because then I'll get a good report. And please help me start to grow up, even if it means my chest has to stick out, which I don't like, but don't forget I'll be fourteen next Christmas.'

NOEL STREATFEILD
A Vicarage Family

Keeping Resolutions

Every man naturally persuades himself that he can keep his resolutions, nor is he convinced of his imbecility but by the length of time and frequency of experiment. This opinion of our own constancy is so prevalent, that we always despise him who suffers his general and settled purpose to be overpowered by an occasional desire. They, therefore, whom frequent failures have made desperate, cease to form resolutions; and they who are become cunning, do not tell them. Those who do not make them are very few, but of their effect little is perceived; for scarcely any man persists in a course of life planned by choice, but as he is restrained from deviation by some external power. He who may live as he will, seldom lives long in the observation of his own rules.

SAMUEL JOHNSON

Lord, when the wise men came from far

Lord, when the wise men came from far,
Led to the cradle by a star,
Then did the shepherds too rejoice,
Instructed by thy angels' voice;
Blest were the wise men in their skill,
And shepherds in their harmless will.

Wise men in tracing nature's laws
Ascend unto the highest cause;
Shepherds with humble fearfulness
Walk safely, though their light be less;
Though wise men better know the way,
It seems no honest heart can stray.

There is no merit in the wise
But love (the shepherds' sacrifice).
Wise men, all ways of knowledge past,
To th' shepherds' wonder come at last;
To know, can only wonder breed,
And not to know, is wonder's seed.

A wise man at the altar bows
And offers up his studied vows
And is received; may not the tears
Which spring too from a shepherd's fears,
And sighs upon his frailty spent,
Though not distinct, be eloquent?

'Tis true, the object sanctifies
All passions which within us rise;
But since no creature comprehends
The cause of causes, end of ends,
He who himself vouchsafes to know
Best pleases his creator so.

When then our sorrows we apply
To our own wants and poverty,
When we look up in all distress

And our own misery confess,
Sending both thanks and prayers above,
Then though we do not know, we love.

SIDNEY GODOLPHIN

Story

For us there are no certainties, no star
blazing our journey, no decisive dream
to reassure hurt hearts or warn us when
it's time to move. The shepherds, harassed men,
are given answers to the questions they
have never thought to ask, told where to go
and what to look for. We try out our way
unlit with angels, wondering 'How far?'
Yet in the story we find who we are:
the baby is told nothing, left to grow
slowly to vision through the coloured scheme
of touch, taste, sound; by needing learns to pray,
and makes the way of the flesh, dark stratagem
by which God is and offers all we know.

JENNIFER DINES

For The Time Being

Well, so that is that. Now we must dismantle the tree,
Putting the decorations back into their cardboard boxes –
Some have got broken – and carrying them up to the attic.
The holly and the mistletoe must be taken down and burnt,
And the children got ready for school. There are enough
Left-overs to do, warmed-up, for the rest of the week –
Not that we have much appetite, having drunk such a lot,
Stayed up so late, attempted – quite unsuccessfully –
To love all of our relatives, and in general
Grossly overestimated our powers. Once again
As in previous years we have seen the actual Vision
     and failed
To do more than entertain it as an agreeable
Possibility, once again we have sent Him away,
Begging though to remain His disobedient servant,
The promising child who cannot keep His word for long.
The Christmas Feast is already a fading memory,
And already the mind begins to be vaguely aware
Of an unpleasant whiff of apprehension at the thought
Of Lent and Good Friday which cannot, after all, now
Be very far off. But, for the time being, here we all are,
Back in the moderate Aristotelian city
Of darning and the Eight-Fifteen, where Euclid's geometry
And Newton's mechanics would account for our experience,
And the kitchen table exists because I scrub it.
It seems to have shrunk during the holidays. The streets
Are much narrower than we remembered: we had forgotten
The office was as depressing as this. To those who have seen
The Child, however dimly, however incredulously
The Time Being is, in a sense, the most trying time of all.
For the innocent children who whispered so excitedly
Outside the locked door where they knew the presents
     to be
Grew up when it opened. Now, recollecting that moment
We can repress the joy, but the guilt remains conscious;
Remembering the stable where for once in our lives
Everything became a You and nothing was an It.
And craving the sensation but ignoring the cause,

We look round for something, no matter what, to inhibit
Our self-reflection, and the obvious thing for that purpose
Would be some great suffering. So, once we have met
    the Son,
We are tempted ever after to pray to the Father:
'Lead us into temptation and evil for our sake'.
They will come, all right, don't worry; probably in a form
That we do not expect, and certainly with a force
More dreadful than we can imagine. In the meantime
There are bills to be paid, machines to keep in repair,
Irregular verbs to learn, the Time Being to redeem
From insignificance. The happy morning is over,
The night of agony still to come; the time is noon:
When the Spirit must practise his scales of rejoicing
Without even a hostile audience, and the Soul endure
A silence that is neither for nor against her faith
That God's Will will be done, that, in spite of her prayers,
God will cheat no one, not even the world of its triumphs.

W H AUDEN
For The Time Being

Twelfth Night

Down from the window take the withered holly.
Feed the torn tissue to the literal blaze.
Now, now at last are come the melancholy
Anticlimactic days.

Here in the light of morning, hard, unvarnished,
Let us with haste dismantle the tired tree
Of ornaments, a trifle chipped and tarnished,
Pretend we do not see,

How all the rooms seem shabbier and meaner
And the tired house a little less than snug.
Fold up the tinsel. Run the vacuum cleaner
Over the littered rug.

Nothing is left. The postman passes by, now,
Bearing no gifts, no kind or seasonal word.
The icebox yields no wing, no nibbled thigh, now,
From any holiday bird.

Sharp in the streets the north wind plagues its betters
While Christmas snow to gutters is consigned.
Nothing remains except the thank-you letters,
Most tedious to the mind,

And the gilt gadget (duplicated) which is
Marked for exchange at Abercrombie-Fitch's.

PHYLLIS MCGINLEY

Ceremonies for Candlemas Eve

Down with the Rosemary and Bays,
   Down with the Mistletoe;
Instead of Holly, now up-raise
   The greener Box (for show).

The Holly hitherto did sway;
   Let Box now domineer;
Until the dancing Easter-day,
   Or Easter's Eve appear.

The youthful Box which now hath grace,
   Your houses to renew;
Grown old, surrender must his place,
   Unto the crispèd Yew.

When Yew is out, then Birch comes in,
   And many Flowers beside;
Both of a fresh, and fragrant kin
   To honour Whitsuntide.

Green Rushes then, and sweetest Bents,
   With cooler Oaken boughs;
Come in for comely ornaments,
   To re-adorn the house.

Thus times do shift; each thing his turn does hold;
New things succeed, as former things grow old.

ROBERT HERRICK

The Ceremonies for Candlemas Day

Kindle the Christmas Brand, and then
   Till Sun-set, let it burn;
Which quenched, then lay it up again,
   Till Christmas next return.
Part must be kept wherewith to tend
   The Christmas Log next year;
And where 'tis safely kept, the Fiend,
   Can do no mischief there.

ROBERT HERRICK

Candlemas in Italy

The parroco came before each Candlemas Day to bless the house. He would walk about it, sprinkling holy water, and he would bring each year a tall and lovely candle of entwined and multi-coloured wax, which he had blessed. We had, too, a number of little candles, made of long spirals of coloured wax twisted close and coiled up like a snake, to be uncoiled as they burned down. They were red and green and yellow and blue, and of great beauty. We took them out with us for our Candlemas picnic, which consisted of oranges, a few preserved fruits, dates and prunes, and fragments of rolls. This feast we took with us along the Savona or the Genoa road, or along the river, or up the hill path behind the house, that climbed, stony and steep, past the carob-tree to our rock houses. Arrived at these craggy piles and promontories, we sat down, lit our coloured candles, and stood them on stones. Rearing slim necks to heaven, they burned, frail and flickering golden buds, while we gnawed bread, sucked oranges, kept the exquisiteness of preserved fruits and French plums for the last *bonne bouche*, and, having finished all, but being still loath to cease, plucked myrtle berries and so prolonged the feast. Some of these were black and plump, almost sweet, others immature and sharp. At any stage, they were better than juniper berries, which dried the mouth.

Thus we kept Candlemas, looking over a wide blue bay through a pink shimmer of almond blossom, while the town below made festa, and a procession wound, harshly chanting, through the deep and narrow streets to Santa Caterina's pink church at the hill's foot. In the still and resinous air our candle-flames burned like little tulips, the flower elongating as the stem dwindled. Thriftily, we would not unwind all the coils and burn them out. The feast done, we extinguished the tapers and put them by for future use. The Candlemas festa thus kept with pious rites, the rock houses became castles to be besieged.

But we had an annual Candlemas difference of opinion with our father, for we thought Candlemas should be a holiday from lessons. Not so he; and he won. So Candlemas Day was wasted until the afternoon.

ROSE MACAULAY
Personal Pleasures

The Child Jesus

Hail, blessed Virgin, full of heavenly grace,
Blest above all that sprang from human race;
Whose heaven-saluted womb brought forth in one
A blessed Saviour, and a blessed son;
O! what a ravishment 't had been to see
Thy little Saviour perking on thy knee!
To see him nuzzle in thy virgin breast!
His milk-white body all unclad, undrest;
To see thy busy fingers clothe and wrap
His spradling limbs in thy indulgent lap!
To see his desperate eyes, with childish grace,
Smiling upon his smiling mother's face!
And, when his forward strength began to bloom,
To see him diddle up and down the room!
O, who would think so sweet a babe as this
Should e'er be slain by a false-hearted kiss!

FRANCIS QUARLES

Mary remembers

Once, measuring his height, he stood
   Beneath a cypress tree,
And, leaning back against the wood,
   Stretched wide his arms for me;
Whereat a brooding mother-dove
Fled fluttering from her nest above.

At evening he loved to walk
Among the shadowy hills, and talk
   Of Bethlehem;
But if perchance there passed us by
The paschal lambs, he'd look at them
In silence, long and tenderly;
And when again he'd try to speak,
I've seen the tears upon his cheek.

JOHN BANNISTER TABB

Has Nothing Changed?

The angel of the Lord appeared to Joseph in a dream and said,
'Get up, take the child and his mother and escape to Egypt.'
(Matthew: 2.13)

> They travelled through the night
> Into Egypt, the stars were clear,
> As they are now,
> The moon was incredibly near,
> The mountains rocky,
> The way dusty,
> As they are now,
> There are those who,
> For one reason or another,
> Travel into Egypt, today.
>
> As the sun came up, cocks crowing,
> It would have become hot,
> The donkey's head would
> Droop lower,
> Ears forward, and the mother
> Would have drawn
> Some shade over the baby's head,
> As they do now.
>
> Into the desert shimmer
> The village they reached
> Would have dozed
> At midday, the old men squatting
> In the shade, and a woman carrying
> A water jar on her head
> Would have greeted them,
> As she greeted me today.
>
> It's a long walk to the well,
> And there is no piped water
> To this village;
> Slowly I seek the shadow of a wall.
> Did the small donkey foal

Out on the glittering sand,
Lick its mother's urine
For moisture then,
As it does now?
Has nothing changed, nothing at all?

MARGUERITE WOOD

Refugee Mother and Child

No Madonna and Child could touch
that picture of a mother's tenderness
of a son she soon would have to forget.

The air was heavy with odours
of diarrhoea of unwashed children
with washed-out ribs and dried-up
bottoms struggling in laboured
steps behind blown emptied bellies. Most
mothers there had long ceased
to care but not this one; she held
a ghost smile between her teeth
and in her eyes the ghost of a mother's
pride as she combed the rust-coloured
hair left on his skull and then –
singing in her eyes – began carefully
to part it . . . In another life this
must have been a little daily
act of no consequence before his
breakfast and school; now she
did it like putting flowers
on a tiny grave.

CHINUA ACHEBE

All in the Morning

It was on Christmas Day,
And all in the morning,
Our Saviour was born,
And our heavenly King:
And was not this a joyful thing?
And sweet Jesus they called him by name.

It was on New Year's Day,
And all in the morning,
They circumcised our Saviour
And our heavenly King:

It was on the Twelfth Day,
And all in the morning,
The Wise Men were led
To our heavenly King:

It was on Twentieth Day,
And all in the morning,
The Wise Men returned
From our heavenly King:

It was on Candlemas Day,
And all in the morning,
They visited the Temple
With our heavenly King:

It was on Holy Wednesday,
And all in the morning,
That Judas betrayed
Our dear heavenly King:
And was not this a woeful thing?
And sweet Jesus we'll call him by name.

It was on Sheer Thursday,
And all in the morning,
They plaited a crown of thorns
For our heavenly King:

It was on Good Friday,
And all in the morning,
They crucified our Saviour,
And our heavenly King:

It was on Easter Day
And all in the morning,
Our Saviour arose,
Our own heavenly King;
The sun and the moon
They did both rise with him,
And sweet Jesus we'll call him by name.

ANONYMOUS

Index of sources and acknowledgements

The editor acknowledges with gratitude the courtesy of the following companies and individuals in permitting the use of copyright material. Page numbers appear in **bold** type.

Achebe, Chinua, *Christmas in Biafra and Other Poems*. Doubleday & Co Ltd. **100, 142**

Andrew, Father, *Love's Fulfilment*. Mowbrays, 1957. **63**

Anonymous, prayers. **3, 67**

Anonymous, *Advent*. **5**

Anonymous, *Yet if His majesty, our sovereign Lord*. **49**

Anonymous, *In Dessexshire as it befel*. **105**

Anonymous, *All in the Morning*. **143**

Anonymous, *The Mirror of Perfection*. **22**

Auden, W H, *Collected Poems*. Faber and Faber Ltd. **132**

Austin, William, *Chanticleer's Carol*. **64**

Bonaventure, St, *The Life of St Francis*. **25**

Bonhoeffer, Dietrich, *Letters and Papers from Prison*, The Enlarged Edition. SCM Press, 1971. **102**

Breton, Nicholas, *Fantasticks*. **83**

Bridges, Robert, *Noel, Christmas Eve, 1913*. **59**

Browning, Robert, *Christmas Eve and Easter Day*. **69**

Burnett, Frances Hodgson, *A Little Princess*. **37**

Calamy, Edmund. **104**

Coleridge, Samuel Taylor, letter from Germany. **27**

Crashaw, Richard, *Come, lovely Name!* **4**

Crashaw, Richard, *Welcome, all wonders in one sight!* **62**

Crashaw, Richard, *Why art thou troubled, Herod?* **117**

Chesterton, G K, *The Illustrated London News 1906*. **6**

Chesterton, G K, *The Illustrated London News 1920*. **13**

Chesterton, G K, *The Thing*. **15, 86**

Chesterton, G K, *The Theology of Christmas Presents*. **20**

Chesterton, G K, *The Contemporary Review 1910*. **20**

Chesterton, G K, *The House of Christmas*. **44**

Chesterton, G K, *G K's Weekly 1933*. **111**

Dickens, Charles, *Christmas Stories*. **32**

Dickens, Charles, *A Christmas Carol*. **71, 107**

Dickens, Charles, *Sketches by Boz*. **85, 103**